COVENTRY

ALSO BY RACHEL CUSK

COVENTRY

Essays

Rachel Cusk

FARRAR, STRAUS AND GIROUX | NEW YORK

Farrar, Straus and Giroux
120 Broadway, New York 10271

Printed in the United States of America
Originally published in 2019 by Faber & Faber Limited, Great Britain
Published in the United States by Farrar, Straus and Giroux
First American edition, 2019

Library of Congress Cataloging-in-Publication Data
Names: Cusk, Rachel, 1967– author.
Title: Coventry : essays / Rachel Cusk.
Description: First American edition. | New York : Farrar, Straus and
    Giroux, 2019.
Identifiers: LCCN 2019020202 | ISBN 9780374126773 (hardcover)
Classification: LCC PR6053.U825 A6 2019 | DDC 814/.6—dc23
LC record available at https://lccn.loc.gov/2019020202

Our books may be purchased in bulk for promotional, educational, or
business use. Please contact your local bookseller or the Macmillan
Corporate and Premium Sales Department at 1-800-221-7945, extension
5442, or by e-mail at MacmillanSpecialMarkets@macmillan.com.

www.fsgbooks.com
www.twitter.com/fsgbooks • www.facebook.com/fsgbooks

10 9 8 7 6 5 4 3 2 1

Contents

I: COVENTRY

Driving as Metaphor

Where I live, there is always someone driving slowly on the road ahead. This is in the countryside by the sea and the roads are narrow and burrow-like, with high hedges either side to protect the fields from the coastal winds. The roads are digressive in character, rarely travelling directly to a specific location. They branch across the flat fields like veins. It is hard to see what's coming, and since there aren't many vantage points it's easy to get lost. Still, it's nothing that requires excessive caution. There's no particular reason for alarm, in fact quite the reverse. Yet people drive at fifteen, twenty, thirty miles an hour. No matter how many of them you get past, there's always another one around the next bend.

A large proportion of these drivers are elderly: their cars are often immaculate and new. At certain seasons there are also many tourists, attempting to manoeuvre their caravans and motorhomes along the winding narrow lanes. There are farms here, and so it is sometimes tractors that block the road, their big churning wheels flinging clods of mud behind them that spatter across your windscreen or land thudding on the car roof. There are stretches where the road briefly straightens so that you can see far enough to overtake. People in big, powerful cars do this boldly and calmly and as though insensible to risk. Others hesitate and miss their chance. But no matter how many times you overtake, within a few minutes you will be stuck behind someone else.

This is a rural area, a backwater, and so it could be assumed that people here are rarely in much of a hurry. Alternatively, it could be said that the relative isolation of our lives can make us less aware of others and of the spaces we share. The coast road is the local thoroughfare: it is usually necessary to take it, to get nearly anywhere you might need to go. It passes through numerous villages whose architecture of narrow bridges and constricted high streets, though scenic, presents many obstacles to the flow of traffic. Problems are constantly arising, and though it could not be said to be the fault of these quaint places, they take on something of the character of an obstacle course when large numbers of vehicles are trying to pass through them. The houses and cottages here are old and have remained the same size, while the vehicles that pass them have become larger: sometimes the cars are no more than two or three feet from their windows. When the traffic is at a standstill, some of the smaller cottages look dwarfed by the cars. It is possible for the people in the cottages and the cars to look at one another.

Several times a day the road through a village will be backed up both ways with stationary traffic, so that it can seem as though there is some calamity or attraction there. Yet it is only the spectacle of people trying to do what they want where it is impossible, for the reason that the vehicles are much bigger and more unwieldy than the humans inside them. At the centre of the jam you will often find, for instance, a giant motorhome and a delivery lorry face to face, unable to get past one another on the narrow village street. This situation can sometimes have no solution other than for one whole line of cars to reverse out of the village to allow the other to pass. If there is no one available to suggest and oversee this operation, the impasse can last a long time. But usually someone assumes the position of author-ity. Trying to unravel these snarl-ups, it often becomes clear that many of its participants are unable fully to manoeuvre and control the cars they are driving. Oth-ers struggle to adapt to the change of circumstance and to the necessity for acting as a group. Passing such a situation on foot, the sight of the rows of human faces trapped behind and framed by their windscreens can be especially striking, as though a portrait-painter had drawn them.

On the open road, the slow drivers often fail effec-tively to communicate their intentions and aims. They will brake for no perceptible reason on a straight and empty stretch, or lose speed until they come inex-plicably to a halt, presumably unaware that there is anyone behind them. If they signal, they do it too late in the build-up to an action; often it is a case of working out what they are doing or mean to do by reading their driving behaviour. A person who slows down at every junction or side road, for example, can be guessed to be looking for a turning but unsure of where it is. Others will brake suddenly when they pass a pub or a shop, evidently considering going in. The usual autonomy and separation of the car, its hermeticism, is reversed: the responsibility of driving, its visual and mental burden, is passed to those outside it. This being a backwater, as well as a place for holidaymakers, it may be the case that people feel entitled to shed that burden here. In this remote place the distinction between private and public worlds is less clear; the contract of the road, its status as a sphere of regulation by agreement, breaks down. Yet there are others for whom this suggestion of lawlessness is the catalyst for signalling their intentions too zealously. They drive as it were sanctimoniously, as though to teach the rest of us a lesson. If they are going to make a right turn, they do it with a great fanfare of long-drawn-out indicating and braking. They obey the rules of the road so deliberately and self-consciously that their behaviour becomes distracting, like actors threatening the integrity of a crowd scene by continually drawing attention to themselves and to the role they are being expected to play. It is as though, for them, the road is not a shared reality but a kind of fiction, an opportunity to become visible through disguise.

*

I have often heard it suggested that elderly citizens should not drive, and that is certainly a consideration where I live. A few years ago a woman of ninety-four killed a girl of ten at a pedestrian crossing. There have doubtless been a number of such incidents, but this one has stayed in my mind. One reason, I suppose, has to do with narrative, with the fact that the meaning of this woman's life was entirely altered by a single event at its end: this is not how stories generally work. Since she had already lived an unusually long life I wondered whether the woman wished she had died before killing the girl, but the question of who is responsible in that situation appears somewhat opaque. One might see the car as a weapon lawfully placed in the driver's hands, in which case a woman of that age ought perhaps to have decided not to drive it; or one might see the laws that leave that decision to her as murderous. The car itself could be viewed as the murderer, since its capacity for destruction is so tenuously linked to that of the person driving it.

The reason most often given by the elderly for continuing to drive is the wish to retain their independence. Without a car, in other words, they would become subject to and entrapped by the reality of their own lives. There are many others for whom this is also the case, people whose arrangements – whether through force of circumstance or as a result of the choices they've made – would be made untenable by having no car. This is a rural area where few services are reachable on foot, so most of the people who live here fall into that category. To have no car, around here, is to be the victim of circumstance.

Several years ago, as the mother of small children and in a different place, I attempted to live without using a car, an undertaking which made every action more effortful in what was already an effortful phase of life. I was not, obviously, trying to make things easier for myself: I was acting as I did out of principle. Something in my situation had made cars unappealing to me. Nearly everything I had to do would have been simplified by using a car, and I believe I saw in this fact a kind of death, as though by taking the easy way out I would miss the opportunity to learn the truth about my situation. Other people were often appalled by this decision and treated its consequences with mockery or anger. There was also a small number of parents who had made the same choice. It was not, largely speaking, a choice made for economic reasons: rather, it appeared to be an ethical response to the fact of parenthood, an attempt to take full responsibility for causing new individuals to exist. These days I often witness the sight of a man or woman on a bicycle with a child and heavy shopping strapped to the back, pedalling furiously through the rain while being overtaken by a stream of cars, or drawn up at a traffic light beside a large clean car with another parent and child sitting calmly inside. The difference between the two is striking without being immediately comprehensible. They might almost be said to represent a mutual criticism; alternatively, they could be seen as demonstrating fundamentally different attitudes to children. If it is true that the cycling parent's behaviour signifies at least the willingness to make greater efforts on behalf of their child, from the outside it can look like the reverse.

Now that my children are grown I drive again, as though my example no longer counts for anything. I remember, from other phases of life, the feeling of freedom and well-being that came from walking or cycling where I needed to go. But around here such behaviour would be impractical: it would be the reverse of freedom, or at least it would appear that way. In the past people routinely walked long distances but now the roads are full of cars. It seems to me that if I walked instead of driving I would make contact with my younger self and with some truth I have forgotten, but to make that decision would almost be to make the fact of oneself too important.

The village where I live is on the coast road, and there is much talk among the residents about how to control the speed at which people drive through it. The slowness that frustrates and impedes us when we are trying to drive on the roads outside the village becomes immaterial from our perspective as homeowners; from this angle, it appears that people around here drive not too slowly but too fast. This might seem merely a good example of the corrosion of truth by point of view. Equally, a person travelling by bicycle feels an antipathy towards cars, yet once inside a car can immediately become irritated by cyclists, and as a pedestrian could dislike them both, sometimes all in the course of a single day. And for those interested in the facts, one aspect of the mystery is easily resolved: the local council has performed numerous speed-testing exercises on the village road and found that the majority of cars passing through are indeed driving in excess of the speed limit.

We accept that we ourselves are guilty of speed-ing thoughtlessly through other people's villages but become sensitive in our own. What is harder to make sense of is our certainty that everywhere other than our own village people drive at speeds so slow they become dangerous. The speed limit inside the village is twenty miles per hour: a car travelling at thirty would be going too fast, yet on the open road thirty can be considered too slow. Is the explanation, therefore, to be found in the inflexibility of people's speeds, their determination to travel at the same pace no matter where they are?

It is not clear to me whether the residents themselves drive too fast through the village. I have often noticed that people go in for the sermonising kind of driving when they are in the vicinity of their own house, par-ticularly if that house is beset by traffic problems: it might be said that they have become disempowered to the degree that their individual example is the only recourse left to them. But equally there can be a feeling of entitlement, of being above the law, on one's own terrain. It has been noted that one person often recognised driving at speed through the village is a member of the parish council, the chief advocate for the imposition of stringent speed restrictions. Where driving is concerned, there seems to be a peculiar difficulty in attaining objectivity: the personal reality of the driver is unassailable, even by his own conscious mind. At the 'Speed Awareness Course' that is the penalty for minor speeding offences, participants are shown a short film in which, asked to concentrate on a particular aspect of the action, they entirely fail to notice a man dressed in a gorilla suit walk across the screen waving his arms and beating his chest. The point we're being asked to accept is that when we drive, what we see is not reality. But what, then, is it?

This is an area of abundant wildlife, and one characteristic of the roads around here is the number and variety of animals that lie crushed everywhere on the tarmac. The bloodied heaps of feathers and fur dry out and decay over time, flattened by the traffic until they become pale two-dimensional shapes that are hard to identify with what they once were. The creatures most commonly killed appear to be the larger game birds – pheasants and quail – that are forever darting out into the road in front of passing cars. The smaller native birds tend to spring away at the sounds of approach but these big ones seem to exist in a state of strange bewilderment, easily panicked and yet without the slightest idea of how to save themselves. If they are standing beside the road, the noise of a coming car will cause them to run directly in its path. The same is true of the small clumsy deer – muntjac – that were introduced to this country in the 1920s from China and have steadily multiplied. Rabbits and squirrels, though quick, are ubiquitous and without particular stratagems and are frequently flattened. Hedgehogs, on the other hand, move so slowly that the question of whether they are crushed or not presumably lies entirely in the hands of fate. Occasionally a stoat or weasel will zoom triumphantly across the road like a funny undulating moustache, too cunning to be caught. A roe deer of considerable size once lay on the verge outside the village for the many weeks it took it to decay, so that every time you passed you saw it at a new stage of this process, the sleeping form still there day after day, visible from some way off.

It is doubtless upsetting to hit a bird or animal and many people swerve to avoid them. Others don't, either because the circumstances would make swerving dangerous or because – whether through indifference or rationality – they don't accept that the responsibility for the situation lies in their hands. The driving scenario, in other words, does not legislate for the behaviour of animals, and so it is not the individual driver's job to avoid them. The car itself, of course, is designed to protect the people inside it, not the objects that cross its path. The airbag that cushions the driver in the event of a collision does not have its exterior equivalent to cushion the thing being collided with. Yet in its weight and hardness, its velocity and power, the car is a more or less invincible aggressor. Nothing soft and living stands a chance against it. When cars were first invented the number of people and animals they hit was proportionately extremely high: the car was not yet a reality that could be anticipated and avoided, to the extent that early cars had to have a person walking in front of them waving a red flag. An analogy might be that if rocks suddenly began falling from the sky, many people would be hit by rocks before they developed systems and strategies to protect themselves. Yet around here at least, these systems are rudimentary compared with the cars' own developments in speed and comfort and passenger safety.

It is often regretted that children can no longer play or move freely outside because of the dangers of traffic; inevitably, many of the people who voice these regrets are also the drivers of cars, as those same restricted children will come to be in their time. What is being mourned, it seems, is not so much the decline of an old world of freedom as the existence of comforts and conveniences the individual feels powerless to resist, and which in any case he or she could not truthfully say they wished would be abolished. There is a feeling, nonetheless, of loss, and it may be that the increasing luxury of the world inside the car is a kind of consolation for the degradation of the world outside it.

In the future, when cars can drive themselves, these feelings of self-division might decrease. The car will become not an extension of the self but its container, and since others will likewise be contained the problems of individuality may recede.

Because of family circumstances, during the past couple of years I've had to drive frequently to the city and back. Emerging from the countryside I am often startled by the ceaseless flow of heavy traffic. It seems incredible to me that so many people could be pursuing their private aims in this public way. But are cars people?

The spectacle of mass movement can look like something unstoppable, yet it is the easiest thing in the world to impede the flow of traffic or to bring it to a halt. On my route there are long stretches of motorway and the traffic is always thickening or lengthening as it meets and then absorbs an obstruction. It doesn't take much for this thickening to become an actual blockage. The sense of embroilment usually comes without any knowledge of what has caused it: often the first sign of it is an increase in awareness of the individual identity of other drivers. The forward-flying host begins to be differentiated: cars that seemed anonymous and distant become closer and more familiar; a web of recognition begins to form itself. The phase of community that follows – lacking any redeeming narrative or central event – is more or less indistinguishable from mutual entrapment. In this context, the difference between a car and a person is not entirely clear. Moments earlier the car was the disguise for, and the enlargement of, the driver's will. Shortly, when the traffic stops, it will become his burden and his prison. But during the phase of transition their mutual relationship seems more biological, a kind of linked separateness.

All sorts of things can cause the traffic to stop, an accident, a scene at the side of the road. It's often surprising how minor these dramas are, compared to the size and extent of their consequences. Their power is cumulative; it arises from the number of people to whom the incident, however trivial, is exposed. I once talked to a man who specialised in patterns of traffic flow and he showed me a set of diagrams illustrating how the merest distraction in one place, something so small that it would cause passers-by to briefly glance at it and therefore unconsciously decrease their speed, could over time result in the whole motorway coming to a standstill in another place miles away.

The drama of the road, once you have been observing and participating in it for a number of years, can be seen to change and develop: new themes arise or die out, new narratives emerge and either progress or fade away again, certain behaviours grow widespread and occasionally take hold. In this country, for instance, the fast lane of the motorway is increasingly full of people driving slowly, while the other two lanes are often more or less empty. On a motorway, it might be said that you ought to know your place: here, increasingly, it is clear that the majority of people – wrongly or otherwise – believe that place to be the fast lane. This belief, and the behaviour that attends it, has numerous consequences, one of which is that it is now almost impossible to get quickly where you want to go. Rather than representing an opportunity for passing, the fast lane is dominated by the person going most slowly, who dictates the speed at which everything behind him is travelling.

As a result, despite the fact that the rules of the road forbid it, people here are now deciding to overtake on the inside. There is some confusion about what this practice should be called: undertaking is – it would seem – the logical formulation, despite its funereal associations. It used to be the case that only reckless or seemingly lawless drivers would undertake, but now a wide range of people can be seen doing it, to the extent that when the traffic is heavy the middle and slow lanes often move faster than the fast one. Undertaking is perceived to be cheating, but the more that people do it, the more it becomes justified as a response to the corruption – as it were – of the principle of the fast lane. The Speed Awareness Course has nothing to say about the question of driving too slowly and the particular dangers it generates, but the undermining of an orderly consensus would seem to be one of them. People decide to take things in their own hands; if there is no longer any fast lane to provide a context for their aims and abilities, they must act for themselves.

Despite the eternal nature of the driving scenario, its boundless time, the mentality of the last chance adheres to it. For example, a car will be driving along a stretch of road with nothing at all behind it and another car will pull slowly out at the last possible moment in front, having watched its approach. It is as though, by approaching, the first driver has caused the second to feel some competition for resources; or as though the second driver can only define himself and his intentions in relation to the first, whom he consequently obstructs. On motorways, often a lorry will abruptly swerve out into the fast lane to overtake another lorry, its size operating as a kind of authority. These incursions can be surprising, even frightening, because the build-up to them is usually hard to perceive. From a distance the lorries seem more or less indistinguishable from one another: their differences in speed are minimal; the reasons for one of them to overtake another are not entirely clear. The drama of this act, being slow to accrue, is therefore unexpected when it comes, but its apparent violence is quickly undermined by the bulk and slowness of the perpetrator. A long line of car drivers quickly builds up behind to watch him inching past a vehicle as slow and cumbersome as his own. When he has succeeded they hurtle by him with contempt. If the difference in speed between the two participants is sufficiently minimal the contest can take a long time and cover many miles of ground, and when this happens the overtaking driver becomes, at a certain point, an aggressor again. His lack of power is having serious consequences: angry as they might be, the cars can't get past him. He has rendered them helpless.

It seems possible that people experience more extreme emotions when they drive, and reveal cruder prejudices, than they might otherwise be aware of or admit to. Perhaps the soldiers of the past, in their suits of armour, felt similarly disinhibited and more capable of violence. Women drivers, for instance, have been openly pilloried, and it is noticeable that even those who would not normally regard themselves as racist or xenophobic frequently describe driving in other places – Germany or Italy or the Middle East – in ways that draw upon or lampoon national characteristics. Road rage, as it is called here, is a common occurrence: people can often be seen shouting or gesticulating at one another from their cars, whereas in the street or other public places such violent outbursts and attacks are rare. Once inside a car it becomes permissible to comment on those outside it, to remark on their appearance or demeanour, with a brazenness absent from most social situations. The occupants of a moving vehicle might even feel licensed to heckle or harass those they see, yet when the car is stripped of its power – by being stopped by traffic lights, for instance, or at a standstill in a traffic jam – and those occupants are exposed, their violence and aggression can rarely be sustained. They may even be frightened of being confronted in the flesh. It has often been observed that people behave in their cars as though they cannot be seen.

Recently, stuck in a traffic jam, I saw an elderly and respectable-looking man leaping wildly and jerkily in his seat, his arms flailing, his face half-demented with anger, shouting things at other drivers that could not be heard through the glass.

Occasionally I meet a person who has never learned to drive. Sometimes he or she is a city-dweller for whom the need to learn has never arisen with sufficient force. Sometimes a lack of opportunity or privilege is the cause. There are also people who appear to have known from the beginning that driving wasn't for them: often they are individuals society might label as sensitive or impractical or other-worldly; sometimes they are artists of one kind or another.

I myself never considered not learning to drive. Had I not learned, my life would doubtless have taken a somewhat different course: I would probably not have been able to live here on the coast, for instance. Yet I don't remember it as having been much of a choice at the time; I don't recall having a sense of the alternatives. But I think about it sometimes, the life I would have lived if I hadn't learned to drive. It might be said that there would have been social and economic consequences to not driving, but for most of the non-drivers I meet that doesn't seem to have been the case. On the contrary, their lives often seem saner and more efficient than my own, more compact, lacking the formless sprawl in personal decisions and arrangements that driving encourages. They are not always, it must be said, above accepting scraps from the driving table, allowing others to ferry them here or there if the need arises. But in the cases that I know of, they have tended to take on fewer responsibilities, to scatter and divide themselves less, to consume and be answerable for a smaller portion of our shared resources. Increasingly I regard them as a kind of elect: they appear, essentially, free. How did they know not to do it?

When I look at my history of driving, I begin to see that it has been analogous to the history of my own will, of all the things I have made happen that wouldn't have occurred naturally on their own. I find myself wondering at the nature of the story it has made up: its relationship to the truth is opaque. My impatience with the slow drivers on these coastal roads, for instance, remains at odds with my fear of cycling on those same roads: perhaps it is myself I am afraid of. Despite my claims to equality, when my husband and I go somewhere together by car I automatically get in the passenger seat. At busy or complicated junctions I find myself becoming self-conscious and nervous about reading the situation: I worry I don't see things the way everyone else does, a quality that otherwise might be considered a strength. Sometimes, stuck on the coast road behind the slow drivers while they decide whether or not they want to turn left, it strikes me that the true danger of driving might lie in its capacity for subjectivity, and in the weapons it puts at subjectivity's disposal. But how can one know when the moment has arrived at which you are no longer capable of being objective?

Recently, hiring a car alone on a trip abroad, I realised that something had changed: the world no longer seemed familiar to me. I struggled to understand the car's controls and its alien shape and size. On the motorway other drivers surged up impatiently behind me, sounding their horns. I had forgotten, it seemed, how to drive; or rather, the degree of responsibility that driving entails suddenly seemed unmanageable to me. Why was everyone else not likewise crippled by this realisation? I moved into the slow lane but lorries loomed in the rear-view mirror one after another and then overtook me, their huge forms seeming about to suck me under as they roared past. On that wide grey unfamiliar road, swept along in the anarchic tumult of speeding cars, every moment all at once seemed to contain the possibility of disaster, of killing or being killed: it was as if driving was a story I had suddenly stopped believing in, and without that belief I was being overwhelmed by the horror of reality. The river of cars plummeted on, relentless and unheeding. But the fact of myself, of my aloneness, had somehow been exposed.

Back at home, rounding a bend on one of the empty roads where I live, I came upon an overturned sports car on the verge. It was a hot summer's day: the upside-down car had its roof down. Lying stiffly beside it amid the foaming white cow parsley were its occupants, a man and a woman, their pale legs sticking straight out in front of them, their shocked faces as rigid as dolls' faces, their summer clothes askew. The man still had his sunglasses on; the woman's broad-brimmed hat lay in the middle of the road. The accident could only just have happened, but no one had seen it and there was no one there.

Coventry

Every so often, for offences actual or hypothetical, my mother and father stop speaking to me. There's a funny phrase for this phenomenon in England: it's called being sent to Coventry. I don't know what the origins of the expression are, though I suppose I could easily find out. Coventry suffered badly in the war: it once had a beautiful cathedral that in 1940 was bombed into non-existence. Now it's an ordinary town in the Midlands, and if it hasn't made sense of its losses, it has at least survived them.

Sometimes it takes me a while to notice that my parents have sent me to Coventry. It's not unlike when a central-heating boiler breaks down: there's no explosion, no dramatic sight or sound, merely a growing feeling of discomfort that comes from the gradual drop in temperature that one might be surprisingly slow – depending on one's instinct for habituation – to attribute to an actual cause. Like coldness the silence advances, making itself known not by presence but by absence, by disturbances of expectation so small that they are registered only half-consciously and instead mount up, so that one only becomes truly aware of it once its progress is complete. It takes patience to send someone to Coventry: it's not a game for those who require instant satisfaction. If you don't live with your victim or see them every day, it might be a while before they even notice they've been sent there. All the same, there's no mistaking this for anything less deliberate than punishment. It is the attempt to recover power through withdrawal, rather as the powerless child indignantly imagines his own death as a punishment to others. Then they'll be sorry! It's a gamble, with oneself as the stakes. My mother and father seem to believe they are inflicting a terrible loss on me by disappearing from my life. They appear to be wielding power, but I've come to understand that their silence is the opposite of power. It is in fact failure, their failure to control the story, their failure to control me. It is a failure so profound that all they have left to throw at it is the value of their own selves, like desperate people taking the last of their possessions to the pawnshop.

But perhaps it isn't like that at all. I remember girls being sent to Coventry at school, a cold and calculated process of exclusion in which the whole cohort would participate. It was a test of an individual's capacity for survival, of her psychological strength: if other people pretend you're not there, how long can you go on believing you exist? This was elemental bullying, the deliberate removal of the relational basis of human reality. The group would watch their victim with interest, as she wandered wordless and unacknowledged through the days. By sending someone to Coventry you are in a sense positing the idea of their annihilation, asking how the world would look without them in it. Perversely, over time, your victim might cultivate exaggerated notions of their own importance, for this troubling fact of their existence seems to have an unusual significance.

Sometimes, at school, a person could ultimately gain power by surviving a visit to Coventry. It is a place of fragments and ruins: I've seen a photograph of the cathedral the day after its bombardment, a few smoking walls standing in an ocean of glittering shards, as if the sky itself had fallen to the earth and shattered. What the image states is that everything, no matter how precious and beautiful, no matter how painstakingly built and preserved, no matter how apparently timeless and resilient, can be broken. That was the world my parents were born into, a world where sacred monuments could disappear between bedtime and breakfast, a world at war: it is perhaps no surprise, then, that war remains their model. War is a narrative: it might almost be said to embody the narrative principle itself. It is the attempt to create a story of life, to create agreement. In war, there is no point of view; war is the end of point of view, where violence is welcomed as the final means of arriving at a common version of events. It never occurred to me that instead of the long siege of sending me to Coventry, my parents might simply have picked up the phone and set things to rights in person. That isn't how stories work. For a start, it's far too economical. The generation of a narrative entails a lot of waste. In the state of war, humans are utterly abandoned to waste in the pursuit of victory. Yet in all the many times I've been sent to Coventry, this question of waste is one I've never really addressed. Sometimes I've been surprised to find myself there again; at other times merely resigned. I've been dismayed, upset, angry, ashamed. I've felt defiant, self-critical, abject; I've gone over and over events, trying to see where I made the mistake, trying to find the crime that might be equal to the punishment, trying to see my own un-acceptability, like trying to see a ghost in the cold light of day. The thing about Coventry is that it has no words: nothing is explained to you there, nothing made clear. It is entirely representational. And what I've never felt about it, I realise, is indifference.

I have a woman friend whose children are starting to leave home. The eldest has gone to university; now the second is filling out application forms, as the others will do in their turn. It's a big family, steady as an ocean liner. There's been no divorce, no disaster; any minor difficulties or discrepancies that have arisen over the years have been carefully toned down and blended back into the picture. Sometimes, talking to my friend, it has occurred to me that even if there had been a disaster, I wouldn't necessarily know about it; that in fact her very definition of a disaster might be 'an event impossible to conceal'. This quality in her, this ability to maintain the surface, has always struck me as a form of courage; indeed, I have vaguely considered her to be the adult in our relationship, though we are more or less the same age. But lately things have changed – or perhaps it would be more accurate to say, since change always implies at least some possibility of renewal, that they have deteriorated. Like an actor coming out of character onstage, there is evidence of slippage, of a loss of frequency in my friend's persona, as though she is losing belief in what she is doing. She has started to talk too much, or not at all, or in non sequiturs; she produces observations out of unfathomable silences, as though laboriously drawing up from the bottom of a well things that have lain there undisturbed for years. It is clear her mind is moving on a different track, away into uncharted distances. One afternoon, at her house, she talks about a feeling she's been having lately – that she'd like to see, piled up in a great mountain, all the things that have been bought and thrown away over the course of their family life. All the toys and the tricycles, the Barbie dolls, the Babygros, the cribs and the chemistry sets, the outgrown shoes and clothes, the abandoned violins and sports equipment, the bright crumpled paper plates from birthday parties, the Christmas trinkets, the souvenirs, the tat from countless gift shops acquired on countless days out, the faddish electronics – everything whose purchase had at the time seemed to offer a solution to something, and whose disposal later on a better solution still: she would like to see it all again, not for the sake of nostalgia but to get the measure of it as objective fact. My friend is admittedly something of a materialist: from the beginning, her enactment of family life was played out amid a substantive and ever-changing set of props. She governed this world of possession with one cardinal rule: every time something new was acquired, something old had to be disposed of. Like a spring of fresh water running through a pond, this mechanism had seemed to avert the danger of stagnation. But now a different possibility appeared to be occurring to her: that it had all been, in the end, a waste.

Stories only work – or so we're always being told – through the suspension of our disbelief. It's never been altogether clear to me whether our disbelief is something that ought to be suspended for us, or whether we're expected deliberately to suspend it ourselves. There's an idea that a successful narrative is one that gives you no choice in the matter; but mostly I imagine it's a question of both sides conspiring to keep the suspension aloft. Being sent to Coventry is perhaps an example of such a conspiracy: it would be hard to send someone to Coventry who refused to believe they were there, just as it's hard to fight a pacifist. Much of my being in Coventry, I now realise, lay in my willingness to recognise and accept the state of being outcast. I suspended my disbelief and having done so I jeopardised, in some sense, my relationship with reality. Like gravity, truth can only be resisted for so long: it waits, greyly, for the fantasy to wear off. My friend's concern with the material evidence of her family life likewise seems to me to be a concern about truth. It is as though each of the many objects that passed through her home over the years represents a lost fragment of reality. She believed in all of it, at the time, believed passionately in the Barbie doll and the violin and the Nintendo that everyone had to have one year – and once the belief had worn off, these things were thrown away. But what, had she not believed in them, might she have seen instead? In the suspension of her disbelief, what did she miss? It is almost as if she feels that the true story of her family has eluded her; and that the mountain of discarded possessions, like a mountain of unopened husks, would represent the size and scale of the mystery.

My husband has observed that two thirds of our conversation is spent discussing our children. He is not the father of my children, and I am not the mother of his. We're like the chief executives of a large corporation: we're in the business of successful management rather than sentimentality. He is careful not to posit this claim as a Bad Thing – it's just a fact, which may or may not be avoidable. Or rather, it's a choice. In choosing to spend two thirds of our time talking about our children, we are perhaps choosing to re-enter the narrative paradigm. We are starting to tell the story again. We are suspending our disbelief.

He doesn't imply that it's my choice more than his,

though history makes that the supposition. In marriage, the woman compensates for her lack of external power by commandeering the story. Isn't that right? She fills the silence, the mystery of her own acts and aims, with a structured account of life whose relationship to the truth might sometimes be described as voluntary. I am familiar with that account: I spent my childhood listening to it. And what I noticed was how, over the years, its repetitions and elisions and exaggerations ceased to exasperate its listeners so much as silence them. After a while, people stopped bothering to try to put the record straight: on the contrary, they became, in a curious way, dependent on the teller of this tale, in which they featured as central characters. The sheer energy and wilful, self-constructing logic of narrative, which at first made one cringe and protest every time the truth was dented, came over time to seem preferable to elusive, chaotic reality.

My husband and I have both come from other marriages: at a certain point our disbelief came crashing down on our heads like the roof of Coventry Cathedral. We live on the coast now, in a village holidaymakers of a certain age like to visit. In the local pub we watch tourist couples sitting in silence over enormous platters of fish and chips. It is unwise, I have learned, to put one's faith in how things look, but it's not often that silence presents itself as a visual event. And other people, it seems, notice the silent couples too. Like the seal colony out on the sound, it turns out they're a sort of local feature. The waiters in the pub treat them with especial tenderness; children gaze at them with what might be wonderment or concern. Our friends discuss them, the men with nervous jocularity, the women with a remote and finely judged pity. Everyone agrees that it is sad. I notice that they are often very well turned out, the woman carefully made up, the man pressed and groomed. They sit erect among the untidy holidaying families with their shoals of tousle-haired children, their dogs, their footballs and frisbees and bicycles, their aura of action and noise as they pass through life like a company of soldiers going over the top. The families are on display – it's part of how they function. Families tend to be conscious of being looked at: they perform themselves as though in expectation of a response, a judgement. I suppose they are exposing what they have created, as an artist feels compelled to do. The exposure ought, in a sense, to correct the subjectivity of parent-hood, though it doesn't always seem to work like that. There are families whose children run through the pub shouting and laughing and knocking over chairs. There are families where the children sit miserably at the ta-ble with downcast eyes while their parents relentlessly chastise them. Jacob, you're annoying the lady, says one mother, mildly and with unmistakable pride, while her son fires his water pistol at another child across my table. Your needs aren't a priority right now, a father is saying at a table on the other side. He is addressing a pallid girl of six or seven, with square-framed glasses and hair in tight, flaxen plaits tied with ribbons. You always get your own way, he adds, raising his glass slowly to his lips.

The silent couples display themselves too, but theirs is an exposure far more mysterious. They sit like monuments, like commemorations of some opaque history: in their silence and their stillness time seems almost to come to a halt. They are like effigies of the dead standing among the living, mute and motionless amid the helter-skelter families and the noise and bustle of the pub. They eat slowly, carefully; they don't, as a rule, look at one another. It is as if, each in themselves, they are alone. I wonder why they have come to this public place to enact their silence. They seem to represent failure: have they come to warn us, like ghosts from purgatory might enjoin us to mend our ways lest we too get caught on the treadmill of our sins? Or have they come just to warm themselves for a few hours with the conversation of others? It could be supposed that they are unhappy, but I wonder whether this is true. Perhaps what they represent is not the failure of narrative but its surpassing, not silence but peace. They are all talked out: this is a notion other people find unsettling. It can be assumed that many of the silent couples have children, now grown up and gone away. What other people don't like, I suppose, is the idea that on the other side of all that effort, all those years of joy and toil and creation, all that suspension of disbelief, there is nothing – or nothing palpable – to look forward to; that one might wake from family life as from a bacchanal into the cold light of day. I wonder whether the silent couples once spent two thirds – or more – of their time talking about their children. I wonder whether their silence represents the problem of reconnecting to reality once the story has ended.

In the day I often walk on the salt marsh, along the coastal path. The marsh is flat and low-lying: from a distance it is merely a strip of grey or brown, banded by the blue line of the sea. It is reached by descending through a copse of trees whose trunks have been sculpted and bleached over time into strange, pale forms by the coastal weather. They glimmer in the copse's half-light like headless bodies held in curious, balletic poses; they are both sensual and unearthly, like a race of nymphs with the glade as their home. The path winds amongst them and out the other side, down to the place where the marsh meets the land. There is always something startling about arriving out of the trees on to the marsh. No matter how much you try to retain its image, the physical sensation of arrival there presents itself anew. It is a feeling of clarity and expansion, as though a word you'd been trying and trying to remember had suddenly come back to you. The marsh has many moods, so it's curious that it delivers these sensations so unfailingly. It is an involuted landscape whose creeks form intestinal patterns amid the springy furze. Twice a day the tide fills these channels silently with water beneath the huge dome of the sky: narrow and deep, they shine like a maze of open cuts. If you try to walk out across it to the sea, you quickly find yourself unable to progress. In Venice, the uninitiated attempt to travel by following their sense of direction and unfailingly get lost, obstructed by the blank walls of culs-de-sac or cut off by a canal with their destination tantalisingly close across the water. Venice obfuscates the notions of progress and self-will, and the marsh does the same. There are paths, but so narrow and faint as to be recognisable only to those who know they are there. The one nearest our house is called the Bait-diggers, the product of years – perhaps centuries – of accumulated knowledge, the knowledge of men who had to trudge across the marsh in all weathers to dig in the distant sands for worms, and who finally iden-tified the merest thread of land that travelled through the sunken archipelago in a more or less straight line from one point to the other. Knowledge is so slender and hard-won, and ignorance so vast and dangerous. Usually I keep to the coast path, a well-travelled route that skirts these tensions. Often I meet the holidaying families there, in their diurnal guises. From a distance, across the flat landscape, they are tiny figures moving untidily but with an overarching logic, like scraps being blown along by a directional wind. They advance slowly but inexorably, scattering and regrouping, occasion-ally pausing as though snagged on some obstacle. As they get closer the pattern becomes more readable and distinct; the figures acquire identity, the story begins to shape itself. They become recognisable as mother, father, children; their movements begin to form the integument of narrative. The scattering and regrouping becomes a meaningful drama of self and others, of human emotion. I watch this drama as it approaches across the marsh, as though on a moving stage. I notice that the adults are often separated: one will walk musingly ahead or behind while the other herds the children along the path. Occasionally they will change roles, like a changing of the guard. The herding parent is released and the solitary muser will rejoin the family reality. I often study the lone parent as they pass, noting the particular quality of their self-absorption. They don't, as a rule, look like people taking in their surroundings: theirs is the self-absorption of someone driving a car through long distances, seeing the world but shut off from it, both free and unfree.

Like any drama, this one involves a lot of talking. I listen to the familiar lines, the cadences of call and response, the river of commentary, the chastisements and encouragements, the opportunities for humour and tension navigated badly or well. The parental script and the script of childhood are more or less adhered to; the performances vary. Excess, the writer Aharon Appelfeld said, is the enemy of art: and it's true that from the outside the family drama is imperilled as a form by the exaggeration of any of its constituent parts, by too much love or too much anger, too much laxity or discipline, too much honesty or not enough. Sometimes, as

I watch, the families cross one or other of these boundaries, and I am struck then by the difference between
the people inside the drama and the people watching.
Often the family actors aren't aware that they've made
their audience wince. I remember once, herding my
small children through Paris, an elegant elderly man
approaching us along the pavement, clearly intending
to speak. I remember wondering what he wanted; I
remember thinking, vaguely, that he might be going to
congratulate us. As he reached me, he raised a long,
slender finger to his lips and made a sshing sound.
Madame, he said, too much noise.

I am a woman of nearly forty-nine, nearly fifty. My
children are teenagers; they spend some of their time
with me and some with their father. The family script
we once followed was abandoned long ago: the stage
was struck; that play is no longer performed. I am conscious sometimes of the fact that no new script has
come to replace it. There have been pilots, synopses,
ideas thrown around; but fundamentally, the future is a
blank. For my children that blank is perhaps subsumed
into the greater question of what and how they will be
in their lives; a patch of thin ice, as it were, at the brink
of a larger and more solid expanse of untried white-
ness. For me, the possibilities are less clear. Throughout my adult life, I have used the need to earn money
as the central support of a sense of self-justification:
as a woman, that always seemed at least preferable to

the alternatives. The need still remains, of course, but increasingly I find it less of a spur. I struggle to suspend my disbelief, but in what? What is there left to disbelieve in?

One weekend, my parents come to stay. It is winter; the coast path is frozen into ruts of black mud and the darkness starts to fall at four o'clock. My husband and I make the house as welcoming as we can. We turn the heating up and put flowers in the rooms. My husband prepares an elaborate meal. When my parents arrive we give them glasses of champagne. But when they leave in their car on a hard and sparkling Sunday morning, I happen to glimpse their faces through the glittering windscreen just before they round the bend and see that their smiles have already vanished and their mouths are moving grimly in talk. I know then that it has happened again: I am going once more to Coventry.

A week of silence passes. My husband is surprised and a little affronted. He had expected a card, a call. He is not familiar with this world in which people accept your hospitality, eat your food and drink your wine and leave with every appearance of bonhomie, then cast you into the outer darkness. Finally he confesses: he believes it is his fault. Late on the last evening, he reminds me, when the dinner had been eaten and the wine drunk, he had brought up the subject of honesty. He had put his arm around me and asked my parents where they thought my honesty had come from. This,

he is now convinced, has caused the rift, though he has
no idea why: but he remembers feeling it, he says, at
the time, a retraction, a jolt in his audience. He blurts
it out like a child who has caused damage by playing
with something he didn't understand; he wishes me to
know it was unintentional.

While his comment may possibly have expedited my
journey to Coventry, I know it wasn't the cause of my
being sent there; yet his remarks have a strange effect
on me. In the following weeks, as the silence grows
and expands and solidifies, I find myself becoming, if
not exactly fond, then increasingly accepting of it. All
my life I have been terrified of Coventry, of its vastness
and bleakness and loneliness, and of what it represents,
which is ejection from the story. One is written out of
the story of life like a minor character being written
out of a soap opera. In the past I have usually been
summoned back after a time, because the scriptwriters
couldn't find a convincing enough reason for my dis-
appearance: a family occasion or social event would
arise whose appearance of normality my absence
would threaten. And I have gone back eagerly, relievedly,
like a dog being let back inside from the cold garden,
for whom the possibilities of freedom are obscured by
the need for acceptance and shelter. Once it has shown
itself unwilling to be free, you can treat that dog how
you like: it won't run away. Sometimes, in Coventry, I
would ponder the idea of freedom. I believed occasionally that I was free. Freedom meant living in Coventry

for ever and making the best of it; living amid the waste and shattered buildings, the desecrated past. It meant waking every day to the realisation that what once existed has now gone. It meant living in the knowledge of waste, of all one's endeavours having been pointless. It meant leaving the story unfinished, like a writer failing to complete the book that, whatever its qualities, has nonetheless been his life's work.

But this time, I start to feel safer in Coventry, safer in the silence. After all, Coventry is a place where the worst has already happened. Theoretically, there should be nothing there to fear. If some kind of accounting is called for, Coventry strikes me as a good place for that to occur. And I wonder whether, if I looked, I would find that other people had decided to come here too; had, as it were, sent themselves to Coventry, searching for the silence, for whatever truth might be found amid the smoking ruins of the story. My friend with her imaginary mountain of tat, for instance, or the silent couples in the pub. Who knows, I might even meet the Parisian gentleman here, and this time impress him with my reticence, my subtlety, my peace.

When I first met my husband I often didn't catch what he said. He spoke too quietly, or so it seemed to me; I'd ask him to repeat himself. He was often silent, and sometimes I found the silences unnerving. They caused me to feel panic: I feared it meant the story was faltering, breaking down; I feared it giving way beneath me. After a while they stopped making me nervous. It even gave me a sense of accomplishment to partici-pate in them: like learning to ride a bicycle, silence was something that looked impossible from the out-side but, once mastered, afforded a certain freedom. It demanded trust, trust in the dynamics. One can't teach someone to ride a bicycle by describing how it's done. A flight into the non-verbal is required. And so I tried it out, silence.

My husband, meanwhile, was trying out talking. After six months or so, he claimed that he had talked more in his time with me than in the whole of his pre-vious life put together. I was struck by the quantity and richness of his vocabulary: it was as if he had opened a vault and showed me his collection of gold bars. I felt glad he'd decided to spend them on me. I have always lived among noisy people, laughers and bellowers, shouters and door-slammers; opinionated people, wits, people who tell good stories. In such company there were words that often got drowned out, shy words like empathy, mercy, gentleness, solicitude. That's not to say they weren't there – it's just that one didn't know for sure, and would forget to look for them in all the noise. My husband uses these words: I sit in Coventry, mulling them over. My parents send him an email, a birthday card, a card for his son; they seem to be inviting him to leave me there and rejoin the story. It seems they now feel they were perhaps a little careless, in how much they chose to waste; they'd like to recoup some of their losses. These approaches make him angry. He was adopted by his own parents as a baby: he does not take abandonment lightly. His father is dead now, but my husband tells me that in the days of their marriage his parents, on the rare occasions they went out for dinner, would often spend the evening in silence. They took pride in it; for them, he said, it signified that their intimacy was complete. When he and I look at the silent couples in the pub, then, we are perhaps seeing different things. My husband doesn't worship silence but he isn't afraid of it either. It is my parents, I begin to understand, who are afraid.

Summer comes: the marsh is dry, and warm underfoot. We take off our shoes to walk to the creek and swim. It is often windy on the marsh. The wind pours out of the flatness and the vastness, from the radial distances where the blue of the sky and the blue of the sea converge. The creek lies between the marsh and the beach, a desolate expanse of sand pockmarked with shells. It is a long, narrow declivity, good for swimming: we remove our clothes, anchoring them against the wind as best we can. I am shy of my body, even in this deserted, primeval space. It is the body of a nearly forty-nine-year-old, but it doesn't feel that way. I have never felt myself to be ageing: on the contrary, I have always had the strange sensation as time passes that I am getting not older but younger. My body feels as though it has innocence as its destination. This is not, of course, a physical reality – I view the proof in the mirror with increasing puzzlement – but it is perhaps a psychological one that conscripts the body into its workings. It is as though I was born imprisoned in a block of stone from which it has been both a necessity and an obligation to free myself. The feeling of incarceration in what was pre-existing and inflexible works well enough, I suppose, as a paradigm for the contemporary woman's struggle towards personal liberty. She might feel it politically, socially, linguistically, emotionally; I happen to have felt it physically. I am not free yet, by any means. It is laborious and slow, chipping away at that block. There would be a temptation to give up, were the feelings of claustrophobia and confinement less intense.

The water in the creek is often surprisingly warm. After the first shock, it is easy to stay in. It is perhaps thirty metres long and I swim fast and methodically up and down. I don't like to talk or mess around when I'm swimming; or it might be more accurate to say that I can't imagine being able to mess around, can't imagine being free from my own rules and ambitions, and more accurate still to say that I'm frightened of what might happen if I were. Instead I set myself a target and count the lengths. My husband dives in and swims for a little while, slowly, without particular direction. Then he turns over and lies on his back and floats, looking at the sky.

*

One day, over the summer, my parents send me an email. They have some furniture they're getting rid of; they wonder whether I want it. I reply, thanking them and declining. A few weeks later, my mother calls and leaves a message. She would like to speak to me, she says. She says she misses the children.

My daughters are an interesting hybrid of characteristics I have always believed to be irreconcilable. They are opinionated, but empathetic too; scarifyingly witty, but capable of gentleness and mercy. They don't waste these finer qualities on adults all that often – friendship is the ground on which they're currently building their lives. But they've been anxious about my presence in Coventry. They aren't familiar with war as the model for human relationships. They aren't used to things remaining fixed enough for the possibility of their destruction to be created. My parents' behaviour has caused them anger, but their forgiveness comes fast after it, like a dog chasing a rabbit: there's barely a beat between accusation and clemency. I'm vaguely aware that something is lost in the speed with which they accept wrongs being set back to rights. Is theirs to be a world without feuds, without lasting conflict, without Coventry, but also without memory? I tell them they are free to communicate with and see their grandparents as often as they please – they are old enough for that to be a reality – but that I myself don't wish to re-enter that arena. I don't want to leave Coventry. I've decided to stay.

They nod their heads, slightly mystified. They don't understand why I care so much. They don't understand why it matters. These are old things, old arguments, old people: it's so much ancient history. It is as though a moss-encrusted monument had suddenly tried to explain itself to them. I say to them, the thing about time is that it can transform the landscape without improving it. It can change everything except what needs to change.

They fidget, roll their eyes, check their phones.

That's really depressing, they say.

My husband and I have a plan, which is to visit certain artworks in the British Isles. I have spent a lot of time looking at art in other places but I have never seen, for instance, Stanley Spencer's paintings in the chapel at Burghclere in Hampshire. I have never visited Henry Moore's house in Much Hadham. I have never laid eyes on Simone Martini's *Christ Discovered in the Temple*, housed in the Walker Art Gallery in Liverpool. We'd like to do a tour that takes all these highlights in.

It's a good idea, though I don't know if it will ever become a reality. It's hard to find the time. There's always something, some new development, some incident or issue, some theme that needs attending to: the story still insists on telling itself, despite our best efforts to block our ears. If it does happen, one place we'll have to go is Coventry. In the aftermath of war, a generation of artists worked to create something afresh in the blasted city. A new cathedral was designed by Basil Spence to stand beside the ruins of the old: Benjamin Britten wrote his *War Requiem* to be premiered at its consecration. Graham Sutherland designed a vast tapestry for the interior; John Piper made the baptistry window, with its nearly two hundred panes; and John Hutton made his expressionist *Screen of Saints and Angels*. People were suspicious, apparently, of the cathedral's modernist design: when what you're used to is irretrievably gone, it's hard to believe in something new. But they suspended their disbelief. The new things came to be, became reality. What needed to change was changed, just as the old things were destroyed – not by time, but by force of human will.

On Rudeness

In a world as unmannerly as this one, how is it best to speak?

In the airport, there are crowds of people at passport control. An official is present: his job is to send them into the right queues. I have been watching him shout at them. I have watched the obsessive way he notices them, to pick on them. When I get close enough, I speak to him.

There's no need to be rude, I say.

His head jerks around.

You're rude, he replies. You're the one who's rude.

This is a place of transit: there are all sorts of people here, people of different ages, races and nationalities, people in myriad sets of circumstances. In this customs hall, there are so many different versions of living that it seems possible no one version could ever be agreed on. Does it follow, then, that nothing that happens here really matters?

No, I'm not, I say.

You are, he says. You're being rude.

The man is wearing a uniform, though not a very impressive one: a white short-sleeved synthetic shirt, black synthetic trousers, a cheap tie with the airport's insignia on it. It is no different from the uniform a bus driver might wear, or someone at a car-rental desk, someone who lacks any meaningful authority while also being forced into constant interaction with members of the public, someone for whom the operation of character is both nothing and everything. He is angry. His face is red, and his expression is unpleasant. He looks at me – a woman of forty-eight travelling alone, a woman who doubtless exhibits some signs of the privileged life she has led – with loathing. Apparently it is I, not he, who has broken the social code. Apparently it was rude of me to accuse him of rudeness.

The social code remains unwritten, and it has always interested me how many problems this poses in the matter of ascertaining the truth. The truth often appears in the guise of a threat to the social code. It has this in common with rudeness. When people tell the truth, they can experience a feeling of release from pretence that is perhaps similar to the release of rudeness. It might follow that people can mistake truth for rudeness, and rudeness for truth. It may only be by examining the aftermath of each that it becomes possible to prove which was which.

The queue moves forward. I reach passport control, and I pass through it, and the man is left behind.

In recounting this incident afterwards, I find myself running into difficulties. For instance, I find myself relying on the details of the man's physical ugliness to prove the badness of his character. Searching for a specific example of someone else's being upset or offended by him, the only person I can prove he offended is me. On another day, a perfectly polite man is probably to be found directing the crowds in the customs hall, assisting the elderly, apologising for the crush, helpfully explaining things to people whose English is uncertain: he would make a good story about individuality as the basis for all hope.

By telling this story, I am trying to substantiate my fear that discrimination and bullying are used against people trying to enter Britain, my country. There are many people who don't have this fear. To them, my story proves only one thing, which is that I once met a rude man in an airport. I might even have inadvertently made them pity him. I, the teller of this tale, would have to demonstrate that under the same circumstances, I would have behaved better. In the event, all I did was criticise him. I made him angrier; perhaps he took it out on the next person in the queue. To top it all off, I admit that he accused me of precisely the same failing: rudeness. Anyone hearing the story will at this point stop thinking about the moral problem of rudeness and start thinking about me. I have damaged my own narrative authority: might I be to blame after all? By including that detail – true though it is – I am giving the man a platform for his point of view. In most of my stories, I allow the truth to look after itself. In this one, I'm not sure that it can.

For all these reasons, the story doesn't work as it should. Why, then, if it proves nothing, is this a story I persist in telling? The answer: because I don't understand it. I don't understand it, and I feel that the thing I don't understand about it – indeed the mere fact of not understanding – is significant.

Another day, another airport. This time the situation is clearer: my country has recently voted to leave the European Union, and rudeness is rampant. People treat one another with a contempt that they do not trouble to conceal. The people in uniforms – the airport officials – exercise their faux power with uncommon ugliness, while the rest of us look suspiciously at one another, not sure what to expect of this new, unscripted reality, wondering which side the other person is on. It is already being said that this situation has arisen out of hatred, but it seems to me that if that is true, then the hatred is of self.

The uniformed woman at security bangs the grey plastic trays one after another on to the conveyor belt with a violence that seems to be a request for attention. At every opportunity, she makes it clear that she has relinquished self-control: her nature has been let loose, like an animal from its cage. She abuses, without exception, every person who passes along her queue, while seeming not to address any single one of them: we are no longer individuals; we are a herd enduring the drover's lash, heads down and silent. She looks unhealthy, her face covered with sore-looking red spots, her shapeless white body almost writhing with its own anger, as though it wishes only to transgress its boundaries, to escape itself in an act of brutality.

The person in front of me in the queue is a well-groomed black woman. She is travelling with a child, a pretty girl with neatly plaited hair. She has put two large clear bags of cosmetics and creams in her tray, but this, apparently, is not allowed; she is permitted only a single bag. The uniformed woman halts the queue and slowly and deliberately holds up the two bags, looking fixedly at their owner.

What's this then? she says. What's this about?

The woman explains that because two of them are travelling, she has assumed that they are entitled to two bags. Her voice is quiet and polite. The little girl gazes ahead with wide, unblinking eyes.

You assumed wrong, the uniformed woman says. Her horrible relish for the situation is apparent. She has been waiting, it is clear, to fasten on someone and has found her victim.

You don't get away with that, she says, grimacing and shaking her head. Where do people like you get your ideas from?

The rest of us watch while she makes the woman unpack the bags and then decide which of her posses-sions are to be thrown away. They are mostly new and expensive-looking. In another situation, their scented femininity might have seemed to mock the ugliness of the woman superintending their destruction with folded arms and a jeering expression on her face. The passenger's varnished fingers are shaking as she scrabbles with the various pots and jars. She keeps dropping things, her head bowed, her lower lip frowning. The uniformed woman's unremitting commentary on these events is so unpleasant that I realise she is half-demented with what would seem to be the combination of power and powerlessness. No one intervenes. I do not inform her that there is no need to be rude. Instead, as I increasingly seem to in such situations these days, I wonder what Jesus would have done.

My travelling companion – a painter – is the politest person I know, but I have noticed that he does not often take up arms on another person's behalf. He dislikes conflict. When it is our turn in the queue, the uniformed woman stares at the bag he has placed in the tray. It contains his tubes of paint. They are crumpled and bespattered with use, and there are so many of them that the bag can't close at the top. She folds her arms.

What are those, she says.

They're paints, he replies.

You can't take those through, she says.

Why not, he asks pleasantly.

The bag has to close at the top, she says. That's why not.

But I need them to paint with, he says.

You can't take them through, she says.

He looks at her in silence. He is looking directly into her eyes. He stands completely quiet and still. The look goes on for a very long time. Her eyes are small and pale blue and impotent: I did not notice them until now. My friend neither blinks nor looks away, and the woman is forced to hold herself there as the seconds tick by, her small eyes open and straining. During those seconds, it seems as if layers of her are being removed: she is being simplified, put in order, by being looked at. He is giving her his full attention, and I watch the strange transformation occur. Finally he speaks.

What do you suggest I do, he says, very calmly.

Well, sir, she says, if you're travelling with this lady, she might have room in her bag.

Neither of them looks at me – they are still looking at each other.

Would that be acceptable? she says.

Yes, he says, I don't see why not.

I proffer my bag, and the woman herself transfers the paints from one bag to the other. Her hands labour to do it with care and exactitude: it takes her a long time. Finally she seals the bag and lays it gently back in the tray.

Is that all right, sir? she says.

Now that he has won this victory, I want him to use it to reprimand her, not just for her behaviour towards the black woman in the queue but for all the wrongs her behaviour represents; for the fact that it's safer to be

him, and always has been. He does not reprimand her.
He smiles at her politely.

Thank you very much, he says.

It would have been a shame to throw them away,
wouldn't it? she says.

Yes, it would, he says. I appreciate your help.

I hope you enjoy your holiday, sir, she says.

Society organises itself very efficiently to punish,
silence or disown truth-tellers. Rudeness, on the other
hand, is often welcomed in the manner of a false god.
Later still, regret at the punishment of the truth-teller
can build into powerful feelings of worship, whereas
rudeness will be disowned.

Are people rude because they are unhappy? Is rudeness like nakedness, a state deserving the tact and
mercy of the clothed? If we are polite to rude people,
perhaps we give them back their dignity; yet the obses-
siveness of the rude presents certain challenges to the
proponents of civilised behaviour. It is an act of disin-
hibition: like a narcotic, it offers a sensation of glorious
release from jailers no one else can see.

In the recollection of events, rudeness often has a
role to play in the moral construction of a drama: it
is the outward sign of an inward or unseen calamity.
Rudeness itself is not the calamity. It is the harbinger,
not the manifestation, of evil. In the Bible, Satan is not
rude – he is usually rather charming – but the people
who act in his service are. Jesus, on the other hand,

often comes across as somewhat terse. Indeed, many of the people he encounters find him direct to the point of rudeness. The test, it is clear, is to tell rudeness from truth, and in the Bible that test is often failed. An un-ambiguous event – violence – is therefore required. The episode of the crucifixion is an orgy of rudeness whose villains are impossible to miss. The uncouth conduct of the Roman soldiers at the foot of the cross, for instance, can be seen in no other light: anyone thinking that Jesus could have done a bit more to avoid his fate is offered this lasting example of humanity's incurable awfulness. They know not what they do, was Jesus' comment on his tormentors. Forgive them.

In the United Kingdom, the arguments rage over the rights and wrongs of the Brexit referendum result. I begin to think this is what it must be like to be the child of divorcing parents. Before, there was one truth, one story, one reality; now there are two. Each side accuses the other, and amid the raised voices, the unappeas-able points of view, the vitriol and distress, the obfus-cation and exaggeration and blame, the only thing that is demonstrably clear is that one side is ruder than the other. It seems to me that even if you didn't know what they were arguing about, you would have to come to that conclusion.

In the aftermath of their victory, the winners are mark-edly unmagnanimous. They brand those who voted the other way as a liberal elite, patronising, self-interested,

out of touch with real life. The liberal elite are characterised as bad losers, as though the vote were a football
match. When they protest against or complain about
the result and its consequences, they are immediately
belittled and shouted down. In the weeks before the
vote, the eventual victors' own handling of language
resembled a small child's handling of an explosive
device: they appeared to have no idea of its dangers
or power. They used phrases like 'We want our country
back' and 'Take back control' that were open to any
and every interpretation. Now they complain that they
have been misrepresented as racist, xenophobic, ig-
norant. They are keen to end the argument, to quit the
field of language where only the headachy prospect of
detailed analysis remains, to take their dubious verbal
victory and run for the hills. They have a blunt phrase
they use in the hope of its being the last word, and it is
characteristically rude: 'You lost. Get over it.'

The liberal elite, meanwhile, have evolved a theory:
it is their belief that many of the people who voted to
leave the European Union now regret their decision.
There is no more tenuous comfort than that which
rests on the possibility of another's remorse. In psycho-
analysis, events are reconstructed in the knowledge of
their outcome: the therapeutic properties of narrative
lie in its capacity to ascribe meaning to sufferings that
at the time seemed to have no purpose. The liberal
elite are in shock; they fall upon the notion of the victors' regret as a palliative for their mental distress, but

because the referendum result is irreversible, this narrative must adopt the form of tragedy.

Unlike the victors, the losers are loquacious. They render the logic of their suffering with exactitude and skill, waxing to new expressive heights. The deluge of fine writing that follows the referendum contrasts strangely with the reticence that preceded it. The liberal elite are defending their reality, but too late. Some urge a show of tolerance and understanding; others talk about the various stages of grief; others still call for courage in standing up for the values of liberalism. These are fine performances, but it is unclear whom they are for. I have often noticed how people begin to narrate out loud when in the presence of mute creatures, a dog, say, or a baby: who is the silent witness to this verbal outpouring?

Meanwhile, in the Essex town of Harlow, a Polish man is murdered in the street by a gang of white youths who apparently heard him speaking his native language.

How can we ascertain the moral status of rudeness? Children are the members of our society most often accused of being rude; they are also the most innocent. We teach children that it is rude to be honest, to say, 'This tastes disgusting' or 'That lady is fat.' We also teach them that it is rude to disrespect our authority. We give them orders: we say, 'Sit still' or 'Go to your room.' At a certain point, I got into the habit, when addressing my children, of asking myself whether I would speak in the same way to an adult and discovered that in nearly every case the answer was no. At that time, I understood rudeness to be essentially a matter of verbal transgression: it could be defined within the morality of language, without needing to prove itself in a concrete act. A concrete act makes language irrelevant. Once words have been superseded by actions, the time for talking has passed. Rudeness, then, needs to serve as a barrier to action. It is what separates thought from deed; it is the moment when wrongdoing can be identified, in time to stop the wrong from having to occur. Does it follow, then, that a bigoted remark – however ugly to hear – is an important public interface between idea and action? Is rudeness a fundamental aspect of civilisation's immunity, a kind of antibody that is mobilised by the contagious presence of evil?

In the United States, Hillary Clinton calls half the supporters of Donald Trump 'a basket of deplorables'. At first the remark impressed me. I approved of Clinton for her courage and honesty, while reflecting on her curious choice of words. 'Basket of deplorables' almost sounded like a phrase from Dr Seuss: it would be typical of him to put deplorables in a basket, for the moral amusement of his young readers. A sack or a box of deplorables wouldn't be the same thing at all, and a swamp of deplorables is too Dante-esque; but a basket is just the kind of zany, cheerful container that makes light of the deplorables while still putting them in their place. It quickly became clear, however, that as a public utterance, the phrase was malfunctioning. The basket began to speak, to distinguish itself: inside it were a number of offended individuals. Clinton had made the mistake of being rude. The 'basket of deplorables' wasn't Dr Seuss after all. It was the snobbish language of the liberal elite, caught committing the elemental moral crime of negating individual human value. Yet Clinton's adversary regularly committed this crime with impunity. Were Clinton's and Trump's two different kinds of rudeness?

In Britain, a man tweets that someone should 'Jo Cox' Anna Soubry. The amorality of the English tongue: in the run-up to the referendum, Jo Cox, a member of parliament, was shot and stabbed to death by a far-right nationalist; to 'Jo Cox' someone is to murder a female member of parliament who advocates remaining in the European Union. The man who posts the tweet is arrested. The police, it seems, are trying to get on top of our verbal problems. It has now become commonplace for proponents of liberal values to receive death threats. The death threat, I suppose, is the extreme of rudeness: it is the point when word finally has to be taken as deed, when civilisation's immunity reaches the point of breakdown. 'I could kill you,' my mother often used to say to me, and I didn't know whether to believe her or not. It is true that I frequently fell foul of her and others through my habit of outspokenness. The sharpness of my phrases maddened her. I was quite capable of the basket-of-deplorables mistake, the confusion of cleverness with insult, the belief in language as an ultimate good, the serving of which was its own reward. No one could mind what you said if you said it with sufficient skill, could they? Later I came to believe that the good of language lay entirely in its relationship to truth. Language was a system through which right and wrong – truth and untruth – could be infallibly identified. Honesty, so long as it was absolute, was a means for individuals to understand all good and evil.

The liberal elite, as far as I am aware, do not make death threats. Is this because they have better manners? Do they in fact wish that their enemies were dead but would just never say so? And if they do wish it – albeit politely, in the manner of a white lie – is the sin somehow less cardinal for being courteous? The anti-liberals do not seem to find their own penchant for death threats problematic. In America, Trump even makes a veiled one against Clinton. We are told by the newspapers that Trump invited the Clintons to his wedding, that their daughters are good friends. Is this verbal violence, then, simply incompetence? Is it the verbal equivalent of someone who has not learned the piano sitting down and trying to play Rachmaninov's Third?

The rudeness of these public figures gives pleasure and relief, it is clear, to their audiences. Perhaps what they experience is not the possibility of actual violence but a sort of intellectual unbuttoning, a freedom from the constraint of language. Perhaps they have lived lives in which they have been continually outplayed in the field of articulation, but of this new skill – rudeness – they find that they are the masters. My mother's death threats undoubtedly arose from her frustration with my own use of language. What I did not take into account when I spoke to her was the difference in our social positions. She was a housewife with little education and a rapidly retreating beauty, for whom life was a process of discovering that no greatness had been held in store for her. She did such things for me as cook and clean, while I was on my way to university and liberty. Yet to my mind, she had an extraordinary power, the power to blacken my mental outlook and ruin my prospect of life. When I spoke to her, I thought I was addressing a tyrant in whose overthrow my only weapons were words. But words were the very things that roused her to violence, because at her life's core, she had been separated from them. Her labour, her maternal identity, her status were all outside the language economy. Instead, she formulated a story of herself whose simplifications and lies infuriated me. I aimed to correct her with truth – perhaps I thought that if only I could insult her with sufficient accuracy, we would be reconciled – but she refused to be corrected, to be chastened. In the end, she won by being prepared to sacrifice the moral basis of language. She didn't care what she said, or rather, she exacted from words the licentious pleasures of misuse; in so doing, she took

my weapon and broke it before my eyes. She made
fun of me for the words I used, and I couldn't respond
by threatening her with death. I couldn't say 'I could
kill you' because it wasn't true, and in language I had
staked everything on telling the truth.

If inequality is the basis on which language breaks
down, how is it best to speak?

In a clothes shop in London, I sift through the rails,
looking for something to wear. The instant I came in,
the assistant bounded up to me and recited what was
obviously a set of phrases scripted by the management.
I dislike being spoken to in this way, though I realise
the assistant doesn't do so out of choice. I told her I was
fine. I told her I would find her if I needed anything. But
a few minutes later, she's back.

How's your day been so far? she says.

The truth? It's been a day of anxiety and self-criticism,
of worry about children and money, and now, to top
it all off, I've made the mistake of coming here in the
unfounded belief that it will make me look nicer, and
that making myself look nicer will help.

It's been fine, I say.

There's a pause in which perhaps she is waiting for me
to ask her about her own day in return, which I don't.

Are you looking for something special? she says.

Not really, I say.

So you're just browsing, she says.

There is a pause.

Did I tell you, she says, that we have other sizes downstairs?

You did, I say.

If you want something in another size, she says, you just have to ask me.

I will, I say.

I turn back to the rails and find that if anything, my delusion has been strengthened by this exchange, which has made me feel ugly and unlikeable and in more need than ever of transformation. I take out a dress. It is blue. I look at it on its hanger.

Good choice, the assistant says. I love that dress. The colour's amazing.

Immediately I put it back on the rail. I move away a little. After a while, I begin to forget about the assistant. I think about clothes, their strange promise, the way their problems so resemble the problems of love. I take out another dress, this one wine-coloured and dramatic.

God, that would look amazing, the assistant says. Is it the right size?

According to the label, it is.

Yes, I say.

Shall I put it in the fitting room for you? she says. It's just easier, isn't it? Then you've got your hands free while you keep browsing.

For the first time, I look at her. She has a broad face and a wide mouth with which she smiles continually, desperately. I wonder whether the width of her smile was a factor in her being given this job. She is older than I expected. Her face is lined, and despite her efforts, the mouth betrays some knowledge of sorrow.

Thank you very much, I say.

I give her the dress, and she goes away. I find that I no longer want to be in the shop. I don't want to try on the dress. I don't want to take my clothes off or look at myself in a mirror. I consider quietly leaving while the assistant is gone, but the fact that I have caused the dress to be put in the fitting room is too significant. Perhaps it will be transformative after all. On my way there, I meet the assistant, who is on her way out. She widens her eyes and raises her hands in mock dismay.

I wasn't expecting you to be so quick! she exclaims. Didn't you find anything else you liked?

I'm in a bit of a hurry, I say.

God, I know exactly what you mean, she says. We're all in such a hurry. There just isn't time to stop, is there?

The fitting rooms are empty: there aren't any other customers. The assistant hovers behind me while I go into the cubicle where she has hung the dress. I wonder whether she will actually follow me in. I pull the curtain behind me and feel a sense of relief. My reflection in the mirror is glaring and strange. I have stood in such boxlike spaces before, alone with myself, and these moments seem connected to one another in a way I can't quite specify. It is as though life is a board game, and here is the starting point to which I keep finding myself unexpectedly returned. I take off my clothes. This suddenly seems like an extraordinary thing to do in an unfamiliar room in a street in central London. Through the gap in the curtain I can see into a dingy back room whose door has been left open. There are pipes running up the walls, a small fridge, a kettle, a box of tea bags. Someone has hung a coat on a hook. I realise that the theatre of this shop is about to break down, and that the assistant's manner – her bad acting, her inability to disguise herself in her role – is partly to blame.

How is everything? she says.

I am standing there in my underwear, and her voice is so loud and close that I nearly jump out of my skin.

How's it going in there? How are you getting on?

I realise that she must be speaking to me.

I'm fine, I say.

How's the fit? she says. Do you need any other sizes?

I can hear the rustle of her clothes and the scraping sound of her nylon tights. She is standing right outside the curtain.

No, I say. Really, I'm fine.

Why don't you come out? she says. I can give you a second opinion.

Suddenly I am angry. I forget to feel sorry for her; I forget that she did not choose to say these things; I forget that she is perhaps in the wrong job. I feel trapped, humiliated, misunderstood. I feel that people always have a choice where language is concerned, that the moral and relational basis of our existence depends on that principle. I wish to tell her that there are those who have sacrificed themselves to defend it. If we stop speaking to one another as individuals, I want to say to her, if we allow language to become a tool of coercion, then we are lost.

No, I say. Actually, I don't want to come out.

There is a silence outside the curtain. Then I hear the rustling of her clothes as she starts to move away.

All right then, she says, in a voice that for the first time I can identify as hers. It is a flat voice, disaffected, a voice that expresses no surprise when things turn out badly.

I put my clothes back on and take the dress on its hanger and leave the cubicle. The assistant is standing with her back to me on the empty shop floor, her arms folded across her chest, looking out the window. She does not ask me how I got on or whether I liked the dress and intend to buy it. She does not offer to take the dress from me and hang it back on its rail. She is offended, and she is very deliberately showing it. We are, then, equal at least in our lack of self-control. I hang up the dress myself.

It wasn't my day, I say to her, by way of an apology.

She gives a small start and utters a sound. She is trying to say something: she is searching, I see, for one of her scripted phrases in the effort to reassume her persona. Falteringly, she half-smiles, but her mouth is turned down at the corners like a clown's. I imagine her going home this evening, unhappy.

When I tell the story afterwards, making myself both its villain and its butt, it goes like this: I, currently dismayed by the sudden ascent of rudeness in our world and wondering what it means, am betrayed into rudeness myself by a personal sensitivity to language that causes me to do the very thing I despise, which is fail to recognise another human's individuality. But the person I tell it to doesn't hear it that way at all. He hears it as a story about how annoying shop assistants are.

I hate it when they do that, he says. It was good you made an issue of it. Maybe she'll give feedback to the management, and they'll stop making people say all that stuff.

What Jesus did was sacrifice himself, use his body to translate word to deed, to make evil visible. While being crucified, he remained for the most part polite. He gave others much to regret. Their regret sustained two thousand years of Christianity. Is regret, then, the most powerful emotion after all?

My mother and I don't speak to each other any more, but I've been thinking about her lately. I've been thinking about facts, about how they get stronger and clearer, while points of view fade or change. The loss of the parent–child relationship is a fact. It is also a failure. It is regrettable. The last time my parents spoke to me, my father said something very rude. He said I was full of shit. He put the phone down straight away after he said it, and I have not heard from him again. For a long time afterwards, I was profoundly disturbed by his words: for my father to speak to me of shit, and claim that I was full of it, seemed to remove my basis for existing. Yet he was half of me: it was, I realised, for that reason that he felt he could speak to me the way he did. I was his child; he forgot that I was as real as he. It could be said that one half of our country has told the other it is full of shit, deliberately choosing those words because it knows that their object finds rudeness – the desecration of language – especially upsetting.

In Sophocles' play *Philoctetes*, the man who suffers most is also the man with the most powerful weapon, an infallible bow that could be said to represent the concept of accuracy. The hard-hearted Odysseus abandoned the wounded Philoctetes on an island, only to discover ten years later that the Trojan War could not be won without Philoctetes' bow. He returns to the island determined to get the bow by any means. For his part, Philoctetes has spent ten years in almost unendurable pain: it is decreed that he cannot be healed other than by the physician Asclepius at Troy, yet he would rather die than help Odysseus by returning with him. Time has done nothing to break down the impasse: Philoctetes still can't forgive Odysseus; Odysseus still can't grasp the moral sensitivity of Philoctetes. It is for the third actor, Neoptolemus, a boy of pure heart, to resolve the stand-off and bring an end to war and pain. Odysseus urges Neoptolemus to befriend Philoctetes in order to steal the bow, claiming it is for the greater good.

Philoctetes, meanwhile, tells Neoptolemus the story of his dreadful sufferings and elicits his empathy and pity. In his dilemma, Neoptolemus realises two things: that wrong is never justified by being carried out under orders, and that the bow is meaningless without Philoctetes himself. The moral power of individuality and the poetic power of suffering are the two indispensable components of truth. For his part, Neoptolemus might be said to represent the concept of good manners. In this drama, the expressive man and the rude man need each other, but without the man of manners, they will never be reconciled.

'Make her stop!' my daughters used to beg me when they were younger and one was doing something the other didn't like. In other words: restore to me the primacy of my version; rid me of this challenge to the experience of being me. One might say that what they wanted was justice, impartiality – but impartiality, I usually discovered, was not easy to attain. There were always two sides to their stories, and I lacked the ability to turn them into one. I have prided myself on my willingness to object to injustices, to speak my mind when I thought I saw wrong being done. But perhaps all I was ever doing was trying to make it stop, trying to return the world to something I could bear to live in, without necessarily understanding it first.

It strikes me that good manners would be the thing to aim for in the current situation. I have made a resolution, which is to be more polite. I don't know what good it will do: this might be a dangerous time for politeness. It might involve sacrifices. It might involve turning the other cheek. A friend of mine says this is the beginning of the end of the global order: he says that in a couple of decades' time we'll be eating rats and tulip bulbs, as people have done before in times of social collapse. I consider the role that good manners might play in the sphere of rat-eating, and it seems to me an important one. As one who has never been tested, who has never endured famine or war or extremism or even discrimination, and who therefore perhaps does not know whether she is true or false, brave or a coward, selfless or self-serving, righteous or misled, it would be good to have something to navigate by.

Making Home

A woman once told me about a visit she made with her husband to an oncologist, to receive the results of his biopsy. She was perhaps in her late sixties, a grandmother, married for forty-odd years. They were kept waiting for a long time, a tense interlude in which she occupied herself with the question of how she would redesign the waiting room if it had to become their permanent home. She had created domestic spaces for so many years, she said, that such thoughts had become a sort of mental tic, a reflexive action she performed to soothe herself. By the time she had resolved the various problems of insufficient light, wrongly positioned doorways and an institutional style of decor, the wait was over and they were called in for their appointment – where, thankfully, she said, the news was better than expected.

As is often the case when people are honest, these remarks struck me as deeply familiar while at the same time creating in me a strong desire to disown them. Not long before, I was driven to what appeared to be the brink of mental and physical collapse by embarking on the complete remodelling of our London flat, and while it was true that my children and I were now

enjoying the benefits of living in a more pleasant environment, I still felt a certain sense of shame at how
determinedly I brought these events about. I caused
walls to be knocked down and floors to be ripped up
and rooms to be gutted; I threw away decades' worth
of clutter and keepsakes and old furniture; with what at
times seemed like magic and at others sheer violence,
I caused the past to be obliterated and put something
new, something of my choosing, in its place. At home,
everywhere I looked I now seemed to see a hidden part
of myself that was publicly exposed: the numberless
private decisions I had made, from the colours on the
walls to the bathroom taps, were exhibited for all to
see. What's more, the very people – my family and
friends – for whom this vision was realised threatened
by their presence to defile it. I flinched when they sat
on the new sofa, and I darted nervous glances at their
shoes strolling imperviously over the unmarked floor;
every scratch and scrape and stain felt as if it were
being inflicted directly to my own flesh. I carped at my
two adolescent daughters for leaving their possessions
strewn over the furniture and berated them for the evidence they left of themselves in the kitchen. At the time
I felt myself to be serving the reality of my domestic
life with them – enhancing it, dignifying it – but now it
almost seemed as if what I really wanted all along was
to erase it.

The 'old' flat had been thickly carpeted in a spongy
brown wool that caused me not the merest flicker of

identification as it underwent the pummellings of daily life; in the cramped kitchen, whose orange-tiled walls and floor gave it something of the dim atmosphere of a butcher's shop, people had happily sat wedged around the table in the murky light on an assortment of chairs and stools of different heights. We had inhabited the old warren of rooms almost with the carefreeness of children, for in a sense those rooms were not ours, not the product of our will or design; yet that same feeling of lawlessness seemed also to create the possibility of getting lost. We were forever searching for one another, calling, wandering from room to room. Sometimes it was hard even to know whether anyone was at home: the thick carpet doggedly absorbed the sounds of life.

We were both more and less ourselves in that undistinguished space, less burdened but less anchored too; freer and yet unreflected, for nothing there gave us back an image of ourselves. When people visited, I felt the need to offer explanations: I would describe what was going to be done to it and what it would look like, as though creating a home out of mere words, and watch their faces brighten as the vision transferred itself from my head to theirs. One day an acquaintance came round, and before I could embark on my tale, he remarked, running his hand fondly over the peeling laminate kitchen counter, on how rare and refreshing it was to be somewhere untransfigured, somewhere of an authentic ugliness that didn't look like a photograph in a magazine or a poor imitation of one. He complimented me on taking this stand against the ubiquity of middle-class tastes; he appeared to view it as an artistic and philosophical position. Don't ever change it, he said with a small smile. I'll be disappointed if you do.

I grew up in a succession of moderately grand houses where the nicest rooms were the ones no one was allowed to use: the drawing room with its dustless ornaments and immaculate cream-coloured sofas, the spare room where the mahogany furniture gleamed and the white bed sheets were always crisp and clean, the study with its unread leather-bound volumes, as forbidding as if it were conserving the memory of someone important who once worked there. Those rooms were full of the tension and silence of a museum: time had stopped there; something above the human had been allowed to take hold. Whom and what were they for? It had seemed ridiculous, but perhaps it was no more ridiculous than the *objet d'art* standing unused in the museum. In their way these rooms were expressive works, attempts to perfect reality and hold it in an eternal moment. They told me something about the person – my mother – who created them. What they seemed to suggest was that she would never be happier than in the home she made for us, at the times when we weren't there.

We moved house often, and each time it appeared that it was the perfecting of our environment that was causing us to leave it, as though living there had been a process of construction that was now complete. In much the same way as an artist's deepest moments of intimacy with a canvas half-consciously generate the need or desire to rid himself of it, my mother perhaps felt a gathering frenzy as she bequeathed her domestic vision to us, for the sight of us starting to make ourselves comfortable there was surely the proof that the picture was finished. The summons of the unknown generally overrides sentiment; possibly, it feeds off it. To continue creating, a person perhaps has to maintain an essential discomfort in the world. The kitchen, where my mother spent most of her time, was often the smallest and dowdiest room in the houses we lived in; and I, too, have found myself working over the years in cramped bedrooms or at the kitchen table, even when a degree of prosperity would have permitted me to claim the much-vaunted room of my own.

In Italy once, I was given a private tour of a beautiful castle, led by the owner through room after impeccably furnished room, only to glimpse at the end through a half-open door a tiny, cave-like space crammed with all the evidence – a gas stove, a television, a tatty sofa – of daily life: this was clearly where the family spent their time. I have often looked at photographs of writers in their elegant book-lined studies and marvelled at what seems to me a mirage of sorts, the near-perfect alignment of seeming with being, the convincing illusion of mental processes on public display, as though writing a book were not the work of someone capable of all the shame and deviousness and cold-heartedness in the world.

One of my daughters has a friend whose house she likes to spend time in. It's a cheerful, comfortable house, always full of people and food. There are the right number of parents in residence and enough attention to go around. It's tasteful and cultured in an unfussy kind of way; the bookshelves are laden, the walls crammed with paintings; there's a dog lying contentedly on the threadbare Persian rug. She can eat on the sofa there, as she can no longer do at home. It looks like a place where people create things, with none of the tensions I associate with creativity: the silence, the solitude, the unappeasable need for the world to disappear so that concentration can occur. For a time I am slightly jealous of her attraction to this household, though I understand it perfectly, for it embodies certain principles of living – generosity, tolerance, the recognition of the human as the pre-eminent value – that I myself hold dear while frequently feeling unable to deploy them in my own home. Like the body itself, a home is something both looked at and lived in, a duality that in neither case I have managed to reconcile. I retain the belief that other people's homes are real where mine is a fabrication, just as I imagine others to live inner lives less flawed than my own. And like my daughter, I, too, used to prefer other people's houses, though I am old enough now to know that, given a choice, there is always a degree of design in the way that people live. The man who admired my peeling Formica was crediting me with, or accusing me of, doing something deliberate, and I don't doubt that the apparent artlessness of my daughter's adopted household is, however half-consciously, a result of a carefully considered set of convictions. That those convictions so closely echo my own makes the illusion – if illusion it is – more tantalising still.

Entering a house, I often feel that I am entering a woman's body, and that everything I do there will be felt more intimately by her than by anyone else. But in that house it is possible to forget entirely – as the passengers on the top deck of a liner can forget the blackened, bellowing engine room below – what is surely nonetheless true: that a home is powered by a woman's will and work, and that a curious form of success could be measured in her ability to suggest the opposite. I can't see any difference, in my daughter's adopted household, between what it is and what it seems to be – the home of a kind, artistic and educated woman – and yet I find myself unable to believe that difference isn't there.

'The house a woman creates is a Utopia,' wrote Marguerite Duras. 'She can't help it – can't help trying to interest her nearest and dearest not in happiness itself but in the search for it.' The domestic, in other words, is ultimately more concerned with seeming than with being: it is a place where personal ideals are externalised or personal failures made visible. These ideals, as well as the forms of failure they create, are ever-changing: the 'search for happiness' is a kinetic state, and it follows that the most seductive of all the illusions of homemaking would be the illusion of permanence.

The novelist Iris Murdoch famously lived in unutterable domestic squalor. She was a philosopher and academic as well as a writer, in the male-dominated intellectual world of Oxford, and I don't doubt that her refutation of domestic servitude needed to be louder and more emphatic than most people's. In that same city, I once visited a family house at Christmastime where the woman was so distressed by the constant human encroachments on the spotless environment she maintained that when someone accidentally dislodged a few needles from the tree, we had to sit there with our feet in the air while she vacuumed them up. Such humiliations can easily be attributed to the transformation of domesticity into a modern psychical event: the suburban housewife with her Valium and her compulsive, doomed perfectionism has been the butt of a decades-long cultural joke. Yet there are other imperatives that bedevil the contemporary heirs of traditional female identity, for whom insouciance in the face of the domestic can seem a sort of political requirement, as though by ceasing to care about our homes we could prove our lack of triviality, our busyness, our equality. Some of the most exacting housekeepers I know are, in fact, men, whose sharing of the care of their children

has led them down the same well-travelled road as
their feminine forebears, for whom the house became
an extension of the self and therefore subject to the
self's same vulnerability, neuroticism and pride. Yet
these men never seem quite so trammelled or devoured
by domesticity, nor so possessed by its utopian visions:
it may be the last laugh of patriarchy that men are better
at being women than women are; but perhaps in relin-
quishing the role of housewife a woman robs it of its
sting, and hands over a neutered identity where a basic
willingness and competence are all that's required. She
walks around with it in her flesh, that sting, the itchy
consciousness of something desisted from, a possibly
harmful habit that leaves an emptiness in its place, like
giving up smoking and not knowing what to do with
your hands.

Another friend of mine runs her house with admirable laxity, governing her large family by a set of principles that have tidiness as a footnote or a distant goal,
something it would be nice to achieve one day, like
retirement. In the kitchen, you frequently feel a distinct crunching sensation from the debris underfoot;
the stairs are virtually impassable with the possessions
that have accumulated there, the books and clothes
and toys, the violins and satchels and football boots,
all precipitously stacked as if in a vertical lost property
office; the children's rooms are so neglected they have
acquired a kind of wilderness beauty, like untouched

landscapes where over time the processes of growth and decay have created their own organic forms. In the kitchen, the children make volcano cakes or create chemical explosions; somewhere in the upper regions of the house, a singing teacher leads the older ones in hollering out show tunes; in the corridors, there is always a multitude of friends and pets and hangers-on milling around. One day a hamster got out of its cage; it was found six months later, living happily with a brood of offspring in a wardrobe. My friend looks at it all with mock despair, then waves it away with her hand. If that's how they want to live, she says, then let them. In this house, the search for happiness appears to be complete; or rather, in the chaotic mountain of jumble it is always somehow at hand, the easiest of all things to find. The foreground is entirely human here: the rooms may have been neglected, but the people haven't been. It is clear to me that by eradicating the tension of the material, my friend has been able to give her children exactly what she wanted to give them – love, authority, the right advice – where for other people these things got mixed up and snagged on one another.

The opposing philosophies of seeming and being, when combined, create a flawed constitution whose rules, if you ever managed to follow them through, ultimately betrayed an alarming lack of logic at their core. How many times had I found myself pursuing bizarre disciplinary arguments in order to uphold domestic laws that possibly I didn't even believe in? I often seemed to see my children looking half-pityingly at me as I railed at them for breaking something or making a mess. Is an object really more important than a person? their eyes seemed to ask. Is tidiness more important than playing? Is there really no difference between an accident – a mistake – and a calculated act of destruction?

Yet for my own mental processes to work, the object-world had to stay still. Objects were capable of exerting an extraordinary mute power: even Virginia Woolf writes in her diary of buying a new chest of drawers and having to leave her writing room every half-hour to go out and look at it. The photograph of the author in his book-lined study represented for me an unattainable ideal, for I would have to be on both sides of the image, creating the stage set and being its principal actor. The artist in me wanted to disdain the material world, while the woman couldn't: in my fantasy of the orderly writer's room I would have to serve myself, be my own devoted housewife. It would require two identities, two consciousnesses, two sets of minutes and hours. One 'I' would have to clear the children's toys from the desk so that the other 'I' could work. The image of the freewheeling mother with her disregard for appearances was somehow threatening from two opposing perspectives, for her apparent inferiority was in fact the reverse: she was superior to the suburban housewife in her miserable prison of immaculate surfaces, and she was superior too to me, to the modern divided woman, because her indifference to the domestic represented a form of courage. With her crunchy kitchen floor and her whirlwind-swept rooms, she was claiming the freedom of a man, or a child, or an artist, at the same time as she was asserting the superiority of her mother-love, for in overthrowing the power of objects she was simultaneously removing them as a last line of defence. Anyone could access her; there was no governed terrain to keep a person out.

I notice one day that my daughter is spending less time with her adopted household. When I ask her about it, she admits that her friend started to comment on her frequent presence there. I feel for her: the provisional home, the home that you are never quite entitled to remain in, is something with which I am familiar. At her age, on Sunday evenings, I had to leave the warmth of the house and be driven through the rain to the train station to go back to boarding school. I wanted only to be allowed to stay where I was; all weekend, the feeling of Sunday evening's approach was as cruel and meticulous as the ticking of a time bomb. The school week had the same cruelty in reverse, as I waited for time to pass the other way and allow me to go home again. Part of the restlessness and anxiety I feel at home has, I realise, to do with time: I am forever waiting, as though home is a provisional situation that at some point will end. I am looking for that ending, that resolution, looking for it in domestic work as I look for the end of a novel by writing. At home I hardly ever sit down: the new sofa has nothing to fear from me. For me, home is not a feeling; it's an image, an idea, a goal, perhaps as it was for my mother, except that – as with so many lost or bankrupt identities – it has filtered down to me as an often inchoate set of tics and compulsions. In their rooms, my daughters drop their clothes on the floor, as though to reassure anyone watching that this history ends with them.

If home was my mother's novel, then we were its created characters, essential but unfree. By contrast I am just a cleaner, a cook, a disgruntled odd-job man: my daughters create themselves. I have tried so hard not to rule them from the baleful matriarchal domestic throne – not to make an awful kind of power out of powerlessness – that I sometimes wonder whether I have done something much worse, which is make myself of no importance. I have played down the domestic work I do as if it were something contagious I don't want them to catch. I have suggested to them that motherhood is a mere scaffolding, a temporary arrangement, like the casing that falls away when the rocket lifts itself from the earth and begins its journey to the moon. After dinner I immediately get up to clear the plates away, and they put out their hands to stop me. Can't we just stay like this for a while? they say.

I have made an unlikely friend, the wife of a long-ago boyfriend. They invite me to their flat for supper; it is on the fourth floor, at the top of a long, winding staircase.

The views are spectacular from inside, and we eat by the window, around their small modern table. At some point during the evening, they ask me if I remember another table, a table I and her husband apparently bought when for a time we shared the flat together. I left that flat – one of many homes I have left – more or less with the clothes I stood up in, too guilty and ashamed to want to take anything with me. The table, along with other things we bought, remained where it was. It was a vast, dark thing made from an enormous slab of wood with a strange carved surface: the top had in fact been the door to a Chinese monastery, and it was mounted on thick dark legs. We bought this gigantic curio from an antiques shop, presumably with the idea of having large dinner parties around it, and though I can't remember those dinners my recollection of the table is entirely clear. It remained in my ex-boyfriend's possession and was still there, in the flat where we now sit, when his wife came on the scene.

Young and jealous then, she set about removing every trace of my existence from what was to become her home. Some of it was easily got rid of; other things – a sofa, a mahogany chest of drawers, a brass bed whose headboard and footboard weighed a ton – required the assistance of removal men. In my abandonment of these things, she perceived some exercise of freedom that she refused to underwrite: if I was going to go, then the whole material world I had created was going to go, too; I couldn't just act as if I were invisible and then leave other people to deal with the concrete facts. The table was the biggest and weightiest of these facts: it was ten or more feet long by four across, and several inches thick; she didn't know how it had ever come up four flights of stairs in the first place. She took a photograph of it and advertised it for sale in the local paper, and before long a young woman phoned wanting to buy it. My friend was at pains to tell her she would need to bring people to help collect it, but the young woman blithely assured her that her boyfriend would probably be around. My friend repeated her injunction that it was a job for several men. It'll be fine, said the young woman, stop worrying.

The evening of the collection arrived. My friend's husband, my ex-boyfriend, had gone away for a week for work, so my friend was alone; it was midwinter and unusually cold. Soon after dark it started to snow, and by the time the young woman rang the bell there was a full-blown blizzard outside. When my friend opened the door and saw the woman standing there unaccompanied – her boyfriend was busy, apparently – she began to despair. The woman – girl, really – was physically tiny, not to mention inappropriately dressed for the task of extracting this colossal incubus, this ten-ton Minotaur, from the fourth floor. Two men happened to be passing on the snowy pavement, and in desperation my friend asked whether they would mind lending a hand; meanwhile the girl had taken out her mobile phone and was tapping at it with varnished fingernails, a process that resulted in a further man arriving shortly afterwards. The team ascended the winding staircase to the flat. The three men could barely lift the tabletop: it was obvious everyone would have to help. My friend rolled up her sleeves, preparing to assist at this great expulsion, like a midwife at a birth. They managed to get it out on to the landing, but it was too large to fit around the corner of the stairs. For an hour or so they manoeuvred it this way and that, but it wouldn't go. Panting, the men began to shake their heads, saying it wasn't going to work. They were ready, it was clear, to give up. But how had the table got there in the first place, if it couldn't come out again? This idea, that I had left behind me something that had grown and impacted itself, something that could never be removed, an inoperable tumour in the heart of her home – inexplicable though it was – galvanised my friend into a state of near-frenzy. Through sheer force of will she held the men to the task. Someone suggested that rather than trying to go round the corners, they lower the table straight down through the gap between the banisters. The drop was some fifty feet; the group formed a sort of human chain, half remaining above to lower the table and half standing below at each level to receive it. At one point the gap between the banisters widened and it was hard for the group below to get a firm hold; my friend, looking down at the scene as though from a great distance, dimly realised that if they lost hold of the table it was entirely possible someone would be killed.

The men were panting and sweating; the tiny girl stood helplessly by, saying, 'Oh, my God' repeatedly. But my friend did not desist; this battle, the battle to drive me out of her territory, was one she was determined to win. With a last excruciating effort the table was lowered to ground level. Breathless and drenched in sweat, my friend walked slowly to the front door and opened it on to the dark, snowy night. The men carried the table out into the white world, and the girl followed them, while my friend remained in the doorway. They were chatting now like old friends; she heard them agreeing to go and have a drink at the pub once they'd put the table in the van. My friend stayed where she was, watching them as they slowly processed away with their dark burden down the pavement through the snow, the sound of their talk and laughter fading while their image remained; an image that reminded her strangely of a funeral procession, the coffin being borne away, the weight of our material evidence being carried out of this life, on the strong shoulders of the pallbearers.

I go to the Lake District for a few days on a walking holiday. In the sunshine on the top of Scafell Pike, my phone rings. It's my sister: she has called to tell me that one of my daughters has had a party at the flat in my absence. More than a hundred people turned up; the disturbance was such that the police were called. I ask if there's been much damage, and there's a long silence before I get a reply.

When I call my daughter, my hands shaking in anger so that I can barely hold my phone, I find myself repeating the same phrases over and over. It's a farce, I keep saying. It's all just a farce. Later I realise that what I was trying to express was the pain of discovering that my narrative of home had been – or so it felt – mocked and rejected. But it does not escape me that the reverse might just as easily be true. To use something, even wrongly, does not have to imply contempt; it might in fact imply belief, belief in the reality of this fabrication, home.

When I get back, I open the door expecting to be hit by the smell of stale alcohol and smoke, but in fact what I smell are flowers. It is a sunny day, and the whole flat is filled with them, roses and irises and hyacinths and daffodils spilling out of every vase and jug that could be found in the cupboards. My daughter has cleaned up; the flowers are her apology. On the journey back, I brooded on the probability that I would never feel quite the same about the home I had created, for while I knew a hundred teenagers had conducted a bacchanal there, the fact that I didn't witness it seemed to create an unbreachable dissociation, a feeling of separation that I was surprised to discover caused me a degree of relief.

I put my bag on the counter and smell the flowers, one after another. I walk from room to room, looking around me like a visitor.

Lions on Leashes

When my two daughters became teenagers, something happened that was unique in my experience of parenting so far: other people began to warn me how awful it would be. Until then, the story of family life that I heard from my contemporaries had been one of relentless – almost frantic – positivism, a bright picture from which shadows were meticulously absent, as though they had been carefully excised. I had struggled to believe in that story, which often seemed to invoke a version of childhood composed of adult fantasies, fantasies so powerful that they threatened to undermine reality itself – a Walt Disney world where wish fulfilment had become a moral good yet whose ultimate desire was to obscure the truth. In my own experience, truth had stubbornly continued to insist on itself: the difficulties of continuing to create while bringing up two small children, the conflict between artistic and familial identity, the attempt to pursue your own truth while still honouring the truth of others, the practical and emotional complexities of motherhood and recently of divorce and single parenthood – all these tensions were real, so real that sometimes their causes were difficult to locate. At such times I learned to recognise the good by its proximity to the bad and vice versa; light and shadow couldn't be separated, for the reason that they defined each other. Yet the public narrative of parenthood denied the light and shadow of reality; it veered insistently, sometimes crazily, towards joy. Sometimes it simply sounded like people trying to bridge the gap – for themselves, as much as for others – between the image and the truth, a gap that is nowhere deeper or more mysterious than in the experience of having a child. But at other times it sounded more like something nobler, something I lacked the knowledge of, a kind of courage or self-restraint that was interwoven with the responsibility of parenthood; a form of election, like knighthood, that brought with it a distinct code of conduct.

Except that suddenly it didn't any more. When people asked me how old my daughters were, they would grimace at my reply. Poor you, they'd say, or, Good luck, or, at best, Don't worry, it'll pass, you'll get them back eventually. Stories began to emerge in my circle of acquaintances, of shouting and slammed doors and verbal abuse, of academic failure, of secrecy and dishonesty; and of darker things, of eating disorders, self-harm, sexual precocity and depression. They used to be so sweet, a friend of mine said of his daughter and son, shaking his head. I don't know what happened. It's like a nightmare. Another friend says, It's as if they hate me. I walk into a room and they wince; I speak and they ball up with irritation. I'm being bullied, she says, reminding me of Raymond Carver's disturbing poem, 'On an Old Photograph of My Son', an outpouring of the author's feelings of victimisation at the hands of his adolescent son, his anger at the waste of his own youth and energy the nurture of this 'petty tyrant' represents. Carver was an artist, and no cheerleader for family life, but perhaps all parents feel an element of artistry in their creation of a child. To be an artist is to have your creation obey you, but as Carver points out, parenthood is the opposite of art: the created object – the child – can become instead an uncontrollable source of destructiveness.

Adolescence, it strikes me, shares some of the generic qualities of divorce. The central shock of divorce lies in its bifurcation of the agreed-upon version of life: there are now two versions, mutually hostile, each of whose narrative aim is to discredit the other. Until adolescence, parents by and large control the family story. The children are the subject of this story, sure enough, the generators of its interest or charm, but they remain, as it were, characters, creatures derived from life who nonetheless have their being in the author's head. A large part of parental authority is invested in the maintenance and upkeep of this story, its repetition, its continued iterations and adaptations. And it feels right to tell it, for what we are offering our children is a story of life in which they have been given a role. How true is it? It's hard to tell. In a story there's always someone who owns the truth: what matters is that character's ability to serve it. But it is perhaps unwise to treasure this story too closely or believe in it too much, for at some point the growing child will pick it up and turn it over in his hands like some dispassionate reviewer composing a cold-hearted analysis of an overhyped novel. The shock of critique is the first, faint sign of the coming conflict, though I wonder how much of what we call conflict is in fact our own deserved punishment for telling the story wrong, for twisting it with our own vanity or wishful thinking, for failing to honour the truth.

My daughters tell me tales of how this conflict is playing out on the other side, in their world. One friend's mother is so fearful for and overprotective of her daughter – an only child – that she won't let her go by train with a group of her friends for a day out; the daughter must remain at home while the others enjoy themselves. Another friend's parents have no idea that their son is a regular and increasingly chronic drug user; they adhere to the happy, sunlit story of family life, while his friends grow more and more anxious on his behalf. Another is subjected to severe and often bizarre penalties and punishments for the minutest failure to achieve excellence in her moral, academic and personal life. Her parents are Catholics, my daughter adds, as though that explained everything.

Because they're told by my daughters, these stories have the teenagers as their protagonists. The stories told by my peers work the other way around. One woman's son texts her abusive messages from his bedroom while she stands cooking in the kitchen below; another's children have defected to live with their father, despite their mother's tireless generosity and care, because he allows them unrestricted access to their phones and laptops; the son of a friend has a party at the family home that results in hundreds of pounds' worth of damage; another's daughter won't invite friends home or allow her parents to pick her up from school because she is ashamed of the family's modest house and car.

I find that I naturally side with the protagonists in my daughters' stories and against the narrators of my friends'. My own memories of adolescence remain the most potent I have. That self is still more real to me than any other I have inhabited. As a thirteen-year-old, I felt both powerless within, and outraged by, the adult world. I was characterised as the family firebrand, the difficult one – but increasingly I find myself recollecting the powerlessness. It is possible, I have discovered, to attribute an inordinate power to your children. But in fact the only power they have is that which lies in the mere fact of existence. They exist: it is from what their existence means for us that the chimera of their power is generated.

I'm currently writing a version of Euripides' *Medea* for a theatre in London. The director and I have an ongoing difference of opinion. The play is notorious for its representation of a woman who kills her two young children; that is what most people know about it, without necessarily being aware of how or why she does so. At its most reductive, Medea is the archetype of the 'bad mother'; vaguely, she has become associated with the concept of maternal ambivalence, in which women's suppressed hatred for and resentment of their offspring is seen as the counterweight to their enactment of 'perfect' motherhood. There is a kind of cultural hysteria around maternal ambivalence that I dislike, for the reason that it takes something subtle and interesting – the mixed feelings of motherhood – and turns it into something blatant and grotesque. The idea that the woman who explores those feelings sits at one end of a trajectory that has child murder at its other is ridiculous. And besides, Medea doesn't kill her children because she dislikes them or finds them irritating. She kills them because her husband has abandoned both her and them for someone young, beautiful and rich. She refuses to be made such use of. She refuses to let him get away with it.

I find that I do not believe in the child-killing as a literal event. But the director cannot conceive of a *Medea* in which the children are not killed. Around this impasse we have arranged ourselves. I say, Ours is a world in which psychological and actual violence have become mutually distinct. The killing no longer means what it once might have. Actual violence is rudimentary and mute; psychological violence is complex and articulate. He says, The play's violence is both metaphor and reality. The two, in other words, meet and mingle, as in the world of Greek mythology, where the gods met and mingled with humans. I say, That metaphor is lost on our literal-minded society; instead the play is regarded as a 'problem play' – but the problem of women murdering their children is not a problem we actually have. Even as metaphor. In fact, if anything, it's the other way around. Metaphorically or otherwise, women don't murder their children. It's the children who murder their mothers.

The director looks sceptical. We discuss the *Oresteia*, in which two children, Electra and Orestes, murder – the former by encouragement and the latter by physical violence – their mother, Clytemnestra. Electra and Orestes aren't, in fact, children. They are teenagers. They hate their mother for the fact that she has disposed of their father. They have come to resent maternal power so much that they destroy it. Instead they reverence the paternal, which is all image – their father, Agamemnon, was away fighting gloriously in Troy for most of their lives – where their mother is all actuality. They crush and disdain that actual parent in pursuit of the imagistic father whose value is recognised out in the world. Sound familiar? I ask.

A writer friend comes round. She brings her son, who is the same age as my older daughter. Once we carried these children in our arms; at other times we pushed them in buggies, or led them by the hand. Now he follows his mother in like a pet lion on a leash, a proud, taciturn beast who has consented, temporarily, to be tamed. My daughter has this same aura of the wild about her, as though beneath a veneer of sophistication she is constantly hearing the summons of her native land, somewhere formless and free that still lies inside her and to which at any moment she might return. The manners of adulthood have been recently acquired. There's no knowing how quickly they could be discarded. She and my friend's son greet each other in territorial monosyllables. It is as though they are two people from the same distant country who have met here in my sitting room. They've met before, often, but you'd never know: those were old versions of themselves, like drafts of a novel the author no longer stands by. All the same, I expect them to take themselves off elsewhere, to another room; I expect them to flee the middle-aged climate of the sitting room, but they don't. They arrange themselves close to us, two lions resting close to the shade of their respective trees, and they watch.

My friend and I have a few years of conversation behind us. We've talked about motherhood – we've both spent a large part of our time as single parents – and its relationship to writing. We've talked about the problems and pleasures of honouring reality, in life and in art. She has never upheld the shadowless account of parenthood; and, perhaps consequently, nor does she now allude to her teenage son as a kind of vandal who has ruined the lovely picture. We talk about our own teenage years, and the hostility of our parents' generation to any form of disagreement with their children. Any system of authority based on control fears dissidence more than anything else, she says; you two don't realise how lucky you are. The lions roll their eyes. What is being controlled, she says, is the story. By disagreeing with it, you create the illusion of victim-hood in those who have the capacity to be oppressors. From outside, the dissident is the victim, but the people inside the story can't attain that distance, for they are defending something whose relationship to truth has somewhere along the line been compromised. I don't doubt that my parents saw themselves as my hapless victims, as many parents of adolescents do ('You have this lovely child,' a friend of mine said, 'and then one day God replaces it with a monster'), but to me at the time such an idea would have been unthinkable. In dis-agreeing with them, I was merely trying to re-establish a relationship with truth that I thought was lost. I may even have believed that my assertions were helpful, as though we were on a journey somewhere and I was trying to point out that we had taken a wrong turn. And this, I realise, is where the feelings of powerlessness came from: disagreement only and ever drew reprisal, not for what was said but for the fact alone of saying it, as if I were telling the residents of a Carmelite convent that the building was on fire and was merely criticised for breaking the vow of silence.

*

In my class at school there was a girl, a sophisticated
creature, clever and sharp-tongued, well dressed,
worldly, mature for her age in body and mind. She
spoke of her mother, with whom she lived, with extraordinary contempt. Her mother was pathetic, a housewife, a drudge. She nagged her daughter to do this or
that; on occasion she overstepped the mark so far as
to obstruct her in the fulfilment of her own plans and
desires. Stupid cow, she would say, arriving at school.
Guess what the bitch has done now? She made these
remarks so often that a kind of story took root in them,
with its concomitant sense of tension that would grow
towards some dark climax. She would come to class
with the latest instalment of the drama, and would relay
the details with scathing laughter. Increasingly her own
role was becoming more active, as though to show us
that she was no victim, that she was about deeds as well
as words. Her mother had berated her for the untidi-
ness of her room, so she had opened her closet and, in
front of her mother, carefully taken everything out and
thrown it on the floor before walking out of the house
to school. Her mother had made some unacceptable
remark over dinner, so she got up from the table with
her plate and emptied the entirety of her meal into the
bin. Her open hatred of this woman mesmerised me.
I was frightened of my own mother, a tense, interior
fear that expressed itself in extreme self-criticism and
doubt, as though she lived inside me and could see
everything that went on there. I could barely see my

schoolmate's mother as a mother at all. Instead I saw
her as something I could not see my own mother as:
a woman, a woman in a kitchen having abuse hurled
at her by this formidable child. And what I remember
most clearly is that this difference – the ability to see
her as a woman – enabled me to pity her.

One day the girl came to school with a slightly wild
and breathless look about her and a glint of triumph
in her eye. On her way out of the house that morning,
her mother had confronted her about something – I
don't remember what – and had blocked her passage
down the hall to the front door, wanting an answer. She
had asked her to get out of the way. The mother had
refused, so her daughter had punched her in the stom-
ach, stepped over her body where it now lay in agony
on the floor and made her way out of the house.

This, in any case, is what the girl said. An adolescent
suddenly finds herself capable of breaking down the
twin fortresses – verbal and physical superiority – of
adult control. She can no longer be physically com-
mandeered, be picked up or constrained; and with that
defence she succeeds in wresting the story of life away
from its authors, or at least in violating the principles
of that story and turning them on their head. Adults
can no longer touch her; she can say what she likes.
When my children were small, I realise now, I routinely used my greater physical strength as a form of
authority. If they wouldn't come when I asked them to,
I could simply go and pick them up. If they wouldn't

sit still, I could hold them still. It all seemed normal and innocent enough, but these days I look back on it with growing amazement. If I had never had access to that brute form of authority, I ask myself, what better authority might I have learned? If I had lacked the arms to pick them up and set them down against their will, to coerce them, would some more platonic parent–child relationship have emerged?

I grew up in a large family where children were treated with all the sensitivity and respect of a herd of animals being corralled by a testy farmer. Respect is something I have had to learn, like French. It feels good to talk in French; the more I speak it the more I improve. But I am also more prone to make mistakes, and to criticise myself for them. When my children reached the first wild shores of adolescence, I felt distinctly the loss of old forms of control: suddenly we had moved into the subjunctive, the past historic, the conditional future. One day, having lunch with my brother, my daughter reached out to take a piece of bread before the meal. I told her to put it back – I wanted her to eat proper food, not bread – and she did, but shortly afterwards she got angry about something else and stormed away from the table. You shouldn't have done that, he said to me. You can't tell her not to eat bread. Would you tell a stranger sitting at the table not to eat bread? He was right: he speaks better French than I. If she'd been smaller, I realised, I'd simply have taken the bread out of her hands. But because of her age – that invisible wall that gradually rises around a person, forbidding trespass – I could no longer do so. However wrong or right it was, all that remained of me from that outdated version of authority were words.

Once, visiting a friend of mine, I watched as he, too, reached the impasse of that physical authority before my eyes: sitting down to lunch, he asked his eleven-year-old daughter to remove her coat and she refused. I'm cold, she said. Take it off, he said. You can't sit at the table in your coat. No, she said. I'm cold, I want to keep it on. He asked her again, and then again, with increasing anger. She wouldn't budge. What was he going to do – strip the coat from her body with his own hands?

Where once we mesmerised our children with our talk – soothing, correcting, steering, but also commanding, naming, judging, apportioning values, calling some things good and others bad, until the whole world had our language on it, a kind of graffiti – now they endeavour to shock us with theirs. We wanted to put them to sleep; they want to wake us up. Inadvertently, often well-meaningly, we fused language with action and thereby created a fundamental confusion, a confusion that is being returned to us in the form of teenagers who have realised they can exist in the space between words and deeds, a space we once denied was there.

My younger daughter attends an all-girls school. She is fourteen and has countless friends, most of them white-skinned and fair, with declarative middle-class voices and abundant shining waterfalls of hair. They move in shoals, around the streets and shops, around the park, talking and shrieking and giggling ceaselessly; their only silences are the dramatic kinds of pauses that occur in the television series they watch, silences that signify the presence somewhere nearby of a narrative event. This event, more often than not, is interpersonal, a plot twist in the politics of their friendship group, a falling-out or change of allegiance, but sometimes it takes the form of a misfortune afflicting one of their number, to whom the rest offer support with hours of murmuring discussion.

Occasionally the shoal drifts in my direction and settles for an afternoon in my house. When my daughter was smaller and invited friends home, I knew I had to provide a narrative explanation of what the afternoon would hold. I made the world known to them by description; almost as if by describing it I created it, or at least maintained control of the narrative: I am mother, you are children, this is home, teatime, play. Sometimes I couldn't bear the conscription of language to this phrase book of false cheer and uniformity; at other times it was soothing to be able to communicate in bland sentences that left my thoughts undisturbed. What was clear, in either case, was that these social rites were a fulcrum of storytelling, a place where a common version of things could be reiterated and agreement reached. The smallest child would know instantly if an adult said something not in the script. They themselves were learning to become scripted, saying please and thank you, answering the questions they were asked. I saw all of us, to a degree, as indoctrinated. In this sphere of universal values, I tried to keep hold of the thread of individuality, yet despite the irritants of this mass religion, the alternatives were unclear.

But now my daughter's friends encounter me in the kitchen, in the hall, with barely a word of greeting. They are silent; they look shiftily to the side. They move on fast, up to my daughter's room, where the sound of talking and shrieking and giggling resumes the instant the door is closed. Quickly they forget I am there; when occasionally they emerge for reinforcements and supplies, they talk in front of me as though I am invisible. Invisibility has at least the advantage of enabling eavesdropping: I listen to them talk, gleaning knowledge of their world. They talk with striking frequency about adults, about the people they now encounter in shops and on buses, the people who serve them in cafes or sell them things. They talk, less mystified, about their teachers. They talk about their grandparents and aunts and uncles. They talk about their fathers, usually with an experimental air of equality, as if they were trying on a pair of shoes that were slightly too big for them. But most of all they talk about their mothers. Their mothers are known as 'she'. When I first heard about 'she', I was slightly puzzled by her status, which was somewhere between servant and family pet. 'She' came in for a lot of contempt, most of it for acts of servitude and attention that she didn't appear to realise were unwanted, like a spurned lover continuing to send flowers when the recipient's affections have moved elsewhere. She's such a doormat, one of them says. When I forget something I need for school, I just text her and she comes all the way across town with it. She's so pathetic. I don't know what Dad even sees in her. Why doesn't she get a job or something?

The talk of these girls brings on a distinct queasiness. I think of the many women I know who agonised over work when their children were small, who curtailed and compromised and very often gave up their careers, sometimes in the belief that it was morally correct and sometimes out of sheer exhaustion. Dad, meanwhile, is revered for his importance in the world. I hear them discuss, with what I am guessing is a degree of exaggeration, their fathers' careers and contacts and the global impact of the work they do; unlike 'she', their fathers are hard-working, clever, successful, cool. They describe them as if they'd only just met them; they describe them as if they'd discovered them, despite the conspiracy to keep these amazing creatures hidden.

When the girls go home, they leave a scene of devastation behind them. The kitchen is strewn with dirty plates and half-eaten food and empty wrappers; the bathroom is a swamp of wet towels, capsized bottles, crumpled tissues smeared with make-up. The smell of nail varnish upstairs is so strong it could knock out a horse. I tidy up, slowly. I open the windows.

Six months later, my younger daughter, I notice, has changed. She has refined her group of friends. There are fewer of them, and the ones that remain are more serious, more distinct. They go to art galleries and lectures together; on Saturdays they take long walks across London, visiting new areas. My daughter has become politicised: at dinner, she talks about feminism, current affairs, ethics. My older daughter has already made this transition, and so the two of them join forces, setting the world to rights. When they argue now, it is about the French headscarf ban in schools or the morality of communism. Sometimes it's like having dinner on the set of *Question Time*. I become aware of their verbal dexterity, their information, the speed of their thought processes. Sometimes I interject, and more often than not am shot down. This, in my own teenage years, would not have been tolerated, yet I find it easy to tolerate. They're like a pair of terriers with a stick: they've got their teeth into the world and its ways. Their energy, their passion, their ferocity – I regard these as the proper attributes of youth. Yet inevitably the argument overheats; one of them storms away from the table in tears, and I have to go and talk her into coming back.

Strange as it may seem, they are still children, still having to operate bodies and minds that are like new, complex pieces of machinery. And indeed, at meal's end, it is I who rises and clears the plates, just as I always have. It would be far too easy to jibe at the skin-depth of their feminism. Besides, I don't see that anything has fundamentally changed in the contract between me and them. For the first time, I am glad of the flaws in our family life, though at times I have suffered bitterly over them, seeing in other people's impeccable domestic lives a vision of stability and happiness I have absolutely failed to attain. But in this new territory, we perhaps have less to lose: no image is being defiled, no standard of perfection compromised. The traditional complaint about teenagers – that they treat the place like a hotel – has no purchase on me. In fact, I quite like the idea. A hotel is a place where you can come and go autonomously and with dignity; a place where you will not be subjected to criticism, blame or guilt; a place where you can drop your towel on the floor without fear of reprisal, but where, hopefully, over time, you become aware of the person whose job it is to pick it up and instead leave it folded neatly on a chair.

One day I go and meet my younger daughter near her school. She left an important book at home. I suggested we meet for lunch so that I could give it to her. I arrive at the agreed-upon place and see that several of her friends are there. Let's go somewhere else, she says, appraising the situation.

The sun is shining. We find a cafe around the corner, a delightful, old-fashioned sort of place, nothing like the crowded chain we originally decided on. The chef, a dapper man with a brown creased head like a walnut, works in full view behind the counter, singing pleasantly to himself in a light tenor. My daughter is happy, happy in the sunshine, happy to see me. I am happy to see her, too. It is as though we have absconded together from that mild prison, home; as though we have got away from what binds us and found each other again on the other side of it, both of us free.

She scrutinises the menu professorially and chooses a chicken salad. I say I'll have the same thing. We talk about her schoolwork, her friends. Lately she has become so independent that watching her live is a kind of spectacle, as though she were walking a high wire with a skill I didn't know she possessed: I watch her from below, proudly, my heart in my mouth.

The chef is making our salads: I see him grilling the slivers of chicken, arranging the leaves, beating a dressing with a tiny silver whisk. He is so quick, so delicate. He bends absorbedly, lovingly over his creation, assembling it, tweaking it with his rapid slender fingers. Carefully, swiftly, he adds the dressing and then with a flourish rings the bell that stands on the counter beside him.

My daughter asks me what I've been doing, what I'm working on, how it's going. At home she rarely asks these questions. At home she is the subject, not I.

I tell her about *Medea* and the problem of the child-killing. I tell her about the Lars von Trier film, in which the older of Medea's children is so helpful that he arranges the noose his mother intends to hang him by around his own neck. In Euripides' version, the children are more palpably her victims, yet they lack distinct personalities of their own. I say, A child might be sacrificed – might even sacrifice himself – to his parents' version of things, just as he might choose to murder his parents' image. But might not all these players be somehow liberated through this violence – cast off their familial identities and be reborn as individuals, as their true selves?

She thinks about this. Among her friends, there are some in serious conflict with parents who continue to insist on the family story. She admits now that her greatest anger at her parents has come from their failure to correspond to the image she has in her head of what a parent should be.

So will she do it? she asks at the end of the lunch. Will she actually kill them?

She's talking about Medea. For an instant I see something in her eyes, a spark of childlike, innocent fear; and she is still, after all, a child. In some respects she always will be.

You'll have to wait and see, I say.

Aftermath

Recently my husband and I separated, and over the course of a few weeks the life that we'd made broke apart, like a jigsaw dismantled into a heap of broken-edged pieces.

Sometimes the matrix of a jigsaw is undetectable in the assembled picture; there are champion jigsaw-makers who pride themselves on such things, but mostly you can tell. The light falls on the surface indentations – it's only from far away that the image seems complete. My younger daughter likes doing jigsaws. The older one does not: she builds card houses in whose environs everyone must remain silent and still. I see in these activities differing attempts to exert control, but I am struck too by the proof they provide that there is more than one way of being patient, and that intolerance can take many forms. My daughters take these variations in temperament a little too seriously. Each resents the opposing tendency in the other; in fact, I would almost say that they pursue their separate activities as a form of argument. An argument is only an emergency of self-definition, after all. And I've wondered from time to time whether it is one of the pitfalls of modern family life, with its relentless jollity, its entirely unfounded optimism, its reliance not on God or economics but on the principle of love, that it fails to recognise – and to take precautions against – the human need for war.

'The new reality' was a phrase that kept coming up in those early weeks: people used it to describe my situation, as though it might represent a kind of progress. But it was in fact a regression: the gears of life had gone into reverse. All at once we were moving not forwards but backwards, back into chaos, into history and prehistory, back to the beginnings of things and then further back to the time before those things began. A plate falls to the floor: the new reality is that it is broken. I had to get used to the new reality. My two young daughters had to get used to the new reality. But the new reality, as far as I could see, was only something broken. It had been created and for years it had served its purpose, but in pieces – unless they could be glued back together – it was good for nothing at all.

My husband believed that I had treated him monstrously. This belief of his couldn't be shaken: his whole world depended on it. It was his story, and lately I have come to hate stories. If someone were to ask me what disaster this was that had befallen my life, I might ask if they wanted the story or the truth. I might say, by way of explanation, that an important vow of obedience had been broken. I might explain that when I write a novel wrong, eventually it breaks down and stops and won't be written any more, and I have to go back and look for the flaws in its design. The problem usually lies in the relationship between the story and the truth. The story has to obey the truth, to represent it, like clothes represent the body. The closer the cut, the more pleasing the effect. Unclothed, truth can be vulnerable, ungainly, shocking. Overdressed, it becomes a lie. For me, life's difficulty has generally lain in the attempt to reconcile these two, like the child of divorce tries to reconcile its parents. My own children do that, forcing my husband's hand into mine when we're all together. They're trying to make the story true again, or to make the truth untrue. I'm happy enough to hold his hand but my husband doesn't like it. It's bad form – and form is important in stories. Everything that was formless in our life together now belongs to me. So it doesn't trouble me, doesn't bother me to hold his hand. There should probably be more hand-holding in the world generally. This was the kind of thing I had started to think.

After a while, time stopped going backwards. Even so, we had regressed quite a long way. In those few weeks, we had undone everything that led to the moment of our separation; we had undone history itself. There was nothing left to be dismantled, except the children, and that would require the intervention of science. But we were before science: we had gone back to something like seventh-century Britain, before the advent of nationhood. England was in those days a country of compartments: I remember, at school, looking at a map of the early medieval heptarchy and feeling a kind of consternation at its diffuseness, its lack of centralised power, its absence of king and capital city and institution. Instead, there were merely regions whose names – Mercia, Wessex – fell effeminately on the ears, and whose ceaseless squabblings and small, laborious losses and gains seemed to lack a driving, unifying force that I might, had I cared to think about it, have identified as masculine.

Our history teacher, Mrs Lewis, was a woman of size and grace, a type of elephant-ballerina in whom the principles of bulk and femininity fought a war of escalation. The early medieval was her period: she had studied at Oxford, and now here she was in the classroom of our mediocre Catholic girls' school, encased in a succession of beige tailored outfits with coordinating heels from which it seemed her mighty pink form might one day startlingly emerge, like a statue from its dust sheets. The other thing we knew about her, from her name, was that she was married. But how these different aspects of Mrs Lewis connected we had no idea. She gave great consideration to Offa of Mercia, in whose vision of a unified England the first thrust of male ambition can be detected, and whose massive earthwork, Offa's Dyke, still stands as a reminder that division is also an aspect of unification, that one way of defining what you are is to define what you are not. And indeed historians have never been able to agree on the question of whether the dyke was built to repel the Welsh or merely to mark the boundary. Mrs Lewis took an ambivalent attitude to Offa's power: this was the road to civilisation, sure enough, but its cost was a loss of diversity, of the quiet kind of flourishing that goes on where things are not being built and goals driven towards. She herself relished the early Saxon world, in which concepts of power had not yet been reconfigured; for in a way the Dark Ages were themselves a version of 'the new reality', the broken pieces of the biggest plate of all, the Roman Empire. Some called it darkness, the aftermath of that megalomaniacal all-conquering unity, but not Mrs Lewis. She liked it, liked the untenanted wastes, liked the monasteries where creativity was quietly nurtured, liked the mystics and the visionaries, the early religious writings, liked the women who accrued stature in those formless inchoate centuries, liked the grass roots – the personal level on which issues of justice and belief had now to be resolved, in the absence of that great administrator civilisation.

The point was that this darkness – call it what you will – this darkness and disorganisation were not mere negation, mere absence. They were both aftermath and prelude. The etymology of the word 'aftermath' is 'second mowing': a second crop of grass that is sown and reaped after the harvest is in. Civilisation, order, meaning, belief: these were not sunlit peaks to be reached by a steady climb. They were built and then they fell, were built and fell again or were destroyed. The darkness, the disorganisation that succeeded them had their own existence, their own integrity; were betrothed to civilisation, as sleep is betrothed to activity. In the life of compartments lies the possibility of unity, just as unity contains the prospect of atomisation. Better, in Mrs Lewis's view, to live the compartmentalised, disorganised life and feel the dark stirrings of creativity than to dwell in civilised unity, racked by the impulse to destroy.

In the mornings I take my daughters to school and mid-afternoon I pick them up again. I tidy their rooms and do laundry and cook. We spend the evenings mostly alone; I do their homework with them and feed them and put them to bed. Every few days they go to their father's and then the house is empty. At first these interludes were difficult to bear. Now they have a kind of neutrality about them, something firm but blank, something faintly accusatory despite the blankness. It is as though these solitary hours, in which for the first time in many years nothing is expected or required of me, are my spoils of war, are what I have received in exchange for all this conflict. I live them one after another. I swallow them down like hospital food. In this way I am kept alive. I live them one after another, processing my sickness, surviving.

Call yourself a feminist, my husband would say to me, disgustedly, in the raw bitter weeks after we separated. He believed he had taken the part of woman in our marriage, and seemed to expect me to defend him against myself, the male oppressor. He felt it was womanly to shop and cook, to collect the children from school. Yet it was when I myself did those things that I often felt most unsexed. My own mother had not seemed beautiful to me in the exercise of her maternal duties; likewise they seemed to threaten, not enhance, her womanliness. In those days we lived in a village in the flat Suffolk countryside; she seemed to spend a great deal of time on the telephone. The sound of her voice talking as though to itself was somehow maddening. Her phrases sounded scripted, her laughter artificial. I suspected her of using a special voice, like an actress. This superficial woman was an impostor – my mother was someone I could never see or hear that clearly. Instead, I seemed to share her point of view, seemed to dwell within her boredom or pleasure or irritation. Her persona was like a second, phantasmagoric house that existed inside our actual house: it was where I lived, unseeing. How could I know what my mother was? How could I see her? For her attention felt like the glance of some inner eye that never looked at me straight, that took its knowledge from my own private knowledge of myself.

It was only when she was with other people that, as a child, I was able to notice her objectively. Sometimes she would have a female friend round to lunch and then all at once there it would be, my mother's face. Suddenly I could see her, could compare her to this other woman and find her better or worse, could see her being liked or envied or provoked, could know her particular habits and her atmosphere, which were not those of this other. At such times her persona, my dwelling place, was inaccessible to me, darkened, like an empty house. If I knocked at the door I was curtly – sometimes roughly – dispatched. Her body, usually so extensive, so carelessly ubiquitous, seemed to have been packed up and put away. And she too was locked out, relieved for a while of the business of being herself. Instead she was performing; she was pure story, told badly or well.

Her friends were generally mothers too, women whose geography I recognised, the sense of an enigma that lay all around their masks of make-up and talk like open countryside around a city. You could never get out into that countryside but you knew it was there. She did have one friend, Jane, who was different from the others. At the time I didn't understand why, but now I do: Jane didn't have children. She was a large woman, a wit, though her face was sad. You could walk around in the sadness of her mouth and eyes; it was open to everyone. She came once when my mother had made a chocolate cake, for which she tried to give Jane the recipe. Jane said, 'If I made that cake I'd just eat the whole thing in one sitting.' I had never heard of a woman eating a whole cake. It struck me as a tremendous feat, like weightlifting. But I could tell that my mother didn't like this remark. In some obscure sense Jane had given the game away. Not knowing any better, she had opened up a chink in the tall wall of womanhood, and given me a rare glimpse of what was on the other side.

Of certain parts of life there can be no foreknowledge – war, for instance. The soldier going to war for the first time does not know how he will behave when confronted by an armed enemy. He does not know this part of himself. Is he killer or coward? When confronted he will respond, yet he doesn't know in advance what his response will be.

My husband said that he wanted half of everything, including the children. No, I said. What do you mean no, he said. This was on the telephone. I looked out of the window at the garden, a rectangle among other urban rectangles, the boundaries prowled by cats. Lately our garden had become overgrown. The beds were drowning in weeds. The grass was long, like hair. But no matter how disorderly it became the grid would be undisturbed: the other rectangles would hold their shape regardless.

You can't divide people in half, I said.

They should be with me half the time, he said.

They're my children, I said. They belong to me.

In Greek drama, to traduce biological human roles is to court the change that is death, the death that is change. The vengeful mother, the selfish father, the perverted family, the murderous child – these are the bloody roads to democracy, to justice. The children belong to me: once I would have criticised such a sentiment severely. Where had this heresy gestated? If it was part of me, where had it lived for all those years, in our egalitarian household? Where had it hidden itself? My mother liked to talk about the early English Catholics forced to live and worship in secrecy, sleeping in cupboards or underneath the floorboards. To her it seemed extraordinary that the true beliefs should have to hide themselves. Was this, in fact, a persecuted truth, and our own way of life the heresy?

I said it again: I couldn't help myself. I said it to my friend Eleanor; that the children belonged to me. Eleanor has a job, is often away for weeks at a time; her husband takes over when she's not there, putting their children to bed, handing them over to the nanny in the morning. Eleanor pursed her mouth and disapprovingly shook her head a little. Children belong just as much to their fathers as to their mothers, she said. I said to my friend Anna, who has no job and four children, the children belong to me. Anna's husband works long hours. She manages the children largely alone, as I now do. Yes, she says, they're your children. You're the one they need. They should be your number-one priority.

It has existed in a kind of banishment, my flesh history with my daughters. Have I been, as a mother, denied? The long pilgrimage of pregnancy with its wonders and abasements, the apotheosis of childbirth, the sacking and slow rebuilding of every last corner of my private world that motherhood has entailed – all unmentioned, wilfully or casually forgotten as time has passed, the Dark Ages on which I now feel the civilisation of our

family has been built. And I was part of that pact of
silence, in a way: it was a condition of the treaty that
gave me my equality, that I would not invoke the primi-
tivism of the mother, her innate superiority, that voodoo in the face of which the mechanism of equal rights
breaks down. My own mother once wept at the supper
table, wildly accusing us of never having thanked her
for giving birth to us. And we joked about it later, cruel
teenaged sophisticates. We felt uneasy, and rightly so:
we had been unjustly blamed. Wasn't it my father who
should have thanked her, for giving form and substance,
continuance, to himself? Instead, his own contribution,
his work, ran parallel to hers: it was she who had to be
grateful to him, superficially at least. For years he had
gone to the office and come back again, regular as a
Swiss train, as authorised as she was illicit. The rationality of this behaviour was what irrationalised hers, for
her womanhood was all imposition and cause, all prof-
ligacy, a kind of problem to which his work was the
solution. How could she expect gratitude for what no
one seemed to think of as a gift? Through her we all of
us served the cause of life: she was the exacting representative of our dumb master, nature. She gave, as
nature gives, but we were not going to survive in nature
on mere gratitude. We had to tame, to cultivate her
gifts; and, increasingly, we ourselves took all the credit
for the results. We were in league with civilisation.

Like God, my father expressed himself through
absence; it was easier, perhaps, to be grateful to some-

one who wasn't there. He too seemed to obey the call of civilisation, to recognise it when it spoke. As rational beings we allied ourselves with him, against the paganism of my mother, her orgies of emotion, her gaze forever dwelling on what was done and past or on the relieving blankness of what was yet to come. These qualities seemed to be without origin: they belonged neither to motherhood nor to herself, but to some eternal fact that arose out of the conjunction of the two. I knew, of course, that once upon a time she had had her own reality, had lived, as it were, in real time. In the wedding photograph that stood on the mantelpiece, her former slenderness was always arresting. There she stood in white, the sacrificial victim: a narrow-waisted smiling beauty, as compact as a seed. The key, the genius of it all, seemed to lie in how little of her there was. In the finely graven lines of her beauty, our whole sprawling future was encrypted. That beauty was gone now, all used up, like the oil that is sucked out of the earth for the purpose of combustion. The world has grown bloated, disorganised, wasteful on oil. Sometimes – looking at that photograph – my family seemed like the bloated product of my mother's beauty.

But for me the notion of a woman's beauty had somewhere in the course of things become theoretical, like the immigrant's notion of home. And in the generational transition between my mother and myself, a migration of sorts had indeed occurred. My mother may have been my place of birth, but my adopted

nationality was my father's. She had aspired to marriage and motherhood, to being desired and possessed
by a man in a way that would legitimise her. I myself
was the fruit of those aspirations but somehow, in the
evolution from her to me, it had become my business
to legitimise myself. Yet my father's aspirations – to suc-
ceed, to win, to provide – did not quite fit me either:
they were like a suit of clothes made for someone else,
but they were what was available. So I wore them and
felt a little uncomfortable, a little unsexed, but clothed
all the same. Both my parents encouraged this form of
cross-dressing, my mother as liable as my father to be
displeased by a bad school report or a mediocre grade,
despite the fact that she herself had no A levels. I got
into Oxford, my sister into Cambridge, egged on by
them both, immigrants to the new country of sexual
equality who hoped to achieve assimilation through
the second generation.

One is formed by what one's parents say and do;
and one is formed by what one's parents are. But what
happens when what they say and what they are don't
match? My father, a man, advanced male values to us,
his daughters. And my mother, a woman, did the same.
So it was my mother who didn't match, who didn't
make sense. We belong as much to our moment in history as to our parents; I suppose it would have been
reprehensible, in Britain in the late twentieth century,
for her to have told us not to worry about our maths,
that the important thing was to find a nice husband

to support us. Yet her own mother had probably told her precisely that. There was nothing, as a woman, she could bequeath us; nothing to pass on from mother to daughter but these adulterated male values. And of that forsaken homeland, beauty, which now lay so despoiled – as the countryside around our Suffolk home was in the years of my growing up despoiled; disfigured by new roads and houses that it pained my oversensitive eyes to look at – of beauty, a woman's beauty, of the place I had come from, I knew nothing at all. I didn't know its manners or its customs. I didn't speak its language. In that world of femininity where I had the right to claim citizenship, I was an alien.

Call yourself a feminist, my husband says. And perhaps one of these days I'll say to him, yes, you're right. I shouldn't call myself a feminist. You're right. I'm so terribly sorry.

And in a way, I'll mean it. What is a feminist, anyway? What does it mean, to call yourself one? There are men who call themselves feminists. There are women who are anti-feminist. A feminist man is a bit like a vegetarian: it's the humanitarian principle he's defending, I suppose. Sometimes feminism seems to involve so much criticism of female modes of being that you could be forgiven for thinking that a feminist is a woman who hates women, hates them for being such saps. Then again, the feminist is supposed to hate men. She scorns the physical and emotional servitude they exact. She calls them the enemy.

In any case, she wouldn't be found haunting the scene of the crime, as it were; loitering in the kitchen, in the maternity ward, at the school gate. She knows that her womanhood is a fraud, manufactured by others for their own convenience; she knows that women are not born but made. So she stays away from it – the kitchen, the maternity ward – like the alcoholic stays away from the bottle. Some alcoholics have a fantasy of modest social drinking: they just haven't been through enough cycles of failure yet. The woman who thinks she can choose femininity, can toy with it like the social drinker toys with wine – well, she's asking for it, asking to be undone, devoured, asking to spend her life perpetrating a new fraud, manufacturing a new fake identity, only this time it's her equality that's fake. Either she's doing twice as much as she did before, or she sacrifices her equality and does less than she should. She's two women, or she's half a woman. And either way she'll have to say, because she chose it, that she's enjoying herself.

So I suppose a feminist wouldn't get married. She wouldn't have a joint bank account or a house in joint names. She might not have children either, girl children whose surname is not their mother's but their father's, so that when she travels abroad with them they have to swear to the man at passport control that she is their mother. No, I shouldn't have called myself a feminist, because what I said didn't match with what I was: just like my mother, only the other way round.

What I lived as feminism were in fact the male values my parents, among others, well-meaningly bequeathed me – the cross-dressing values of my father, and the anti-feminine values of my mother. So I am not a feminist. I am a self-hating transvestite.

Like many women I know, I have never been supported financially by a man. This is anecdotal information – women have a weakness for that. And perhaps a feminist is someone who possesses this personalising trait to a larger-than-average degree: she is an autobiographer, an artist of the self. She acts as an interface between private and public, just as women always have, except that the feminist does it in reverse. She does not propitiate: she objects. She's a woman turned inside out.

If you live long enough, the anecdotal becomes the statistical in any case. You emerge with your cohorts out of the jungle of middle life, each possessing your own private knowledge of courage or cowardice, and do a quick headcount, an inventory of missing limbs. I know women with four children and women with no children, divorced women and married women, successful and compromised women, apologetic, ambitious and contented women, women who are unfulfilled or accepting, selfless and frustrated women. And some of them, it is true, are not financially dependent on men. What can I say about the ones that are? That they're usually full-time mothers. And that they live more through their children. That's how it seems to me. The child goes through the full-time mother like a dye through water: there is no part of her that remains uncoloured. The child's triumphs and losses are her triumphs and losses. The child's beauty is her beauty, as is the child's unacceptability. And because management of the child is her job, her own management of the world is conducted through it. Her subjectivity has more than one source, and only a single outlet. This can result in extreme competence: some of my friends claim to find such women frightening or threatening. These friends are generally women who sustain more than one identity out of a single self, and hence perhaps fear accusations of extreme incompetence. Their power is diffuse: they never feel it collected in one place, and as a result they don't know how much of it there is, whether they have less or more power than that curiously titled creature, the stay-at-home mum, or indeed than their male colleagues at work who must, I suppose, share at least some of their feelings of scatteration.

A few of these working-mother friends of mine have taken the occasional domestic furlough, usually in the early years of parenthood. Like wanted criminals finally run to ground, they surrender with their hands up: yes, it was all too much, too unworkable, the running hither and thither, the guilt, the pressure at work, the pressure at home, the question of why – if you were never going to see them – you went to the trouble of having children in the first place. So they decide to stay at home for a year or two and even things up a bit, like the cake mixture the recipe tells you to divide between two tins, of which there always seems to be more in one than the other. Their husbands also work, live in the same houses and parent the same children, yet don't seem to experience quite the same measure of conflict. In fact, sometimes they actually look like they're better at being working parents than women are – insufferable male superiority!

But a man commits no particular heresy against his sex by being a good father, and working is part of what a good father does. The working mother, on the other hand, is traducing her role in the founding myths of civilisation on a daily basis – no wonder she's a little harassed. She's trying to defy her own deep-seated rela-tionship with gravity. I read somewhere that a space station is always slowly falling back to Earth, and that every few months or so a rocket has to be sent to push it back out again. In rather the same way, a woman is for-ever dragged at by an imperceptible force of biological conformism: her life is relentlessly iterative; it requires energy to keep her in orbit. Year after year she'll do it, but if one year the rocket doesn't come then down she'll go.

The stay-at-home mum often describes herself as lucky: that's her pitch, her line, should anyone – a working mother, for instance – care to enquire. We're so lucky that James's salary means I don't have to work, she'll say, as though she took a huge punt on a single horse and found that she'd backed a winner. You don't catch a man saying he feels lucky to be able to go to the office every day. Yet the stay-at-home mum often calls it a privilege, to be 'allowed' to do her traditional and entirely unexceptional domestic work. It's a defensive statement, of course – she doesn't want to be thought of as lazy or unambitious – and like much defensiveness it (barely) conceals a core of aggression. Yet presumably she is elated when her daughter comes top in the maths test, gets a place at Cambridge, becomes a nuclear physicist. Does she wish it for her daughter, that privilege, the time-immemorial life at home with children? Or does she think this is a riddle that someone in the future will somehow just solve, like scientists inventing the cure for cancer?

I remember, when my own children were born, when I first held them and fed them and talked to them, feeling a great awareness of this new, foreign aspect of myself that was in me and yet did not seem to be of me. It was as though I had suddenly acquired the ability to speak Russian: what I could do – this women's work – had so much form of its own, yet I didn't know where my knowledge of it had come from. In some ways I wanted to claim the knowledge as mine, as innate, but to do that seemed to involve a strange kind of dishonesty, a pretending. And yet, how could I pretend to be what I already was? I felt inhabited by a second self, a twin whose jest it was – in the way of twins – to appear to be me while doing things that were alien to my own character. Yet this twin was not apparently malign: she was just asking for a degree of freedom, a temporary release from the strict protocol of identity. She wanted to act as a woman, a generic woman, but character is not generic. It is entirely and utterly specific. To act as a mother, I had to suspend my own character, which had evolved on a diet of male values. And my habitat, my environment, had evolved that way too. An adaptation would be required. But who was going to do the adapting? I was aware, in those early days, that my behaviour was strange to the people who knew me well. It was as though I had been brainwashed, taken over by a cult religion. I had gone away – I couldn't be reached on the usual number. And yet this cult, motherhood, was not a place where I could actually live. It reflected nothing about me: its literature and practices, its values, its codes of conduct, its aesthetic were not mine. It was generic too: like any cult, it demanded a complete surrender of identity to belong to it. So for a while I didn't belong anywhere. As the mother of young children I was homeless, drifting, itinerant. And I felt an inadmissible pity for myself and for my daughters in those years. It seemed almost catastrophic to me, the disenchantment of this contact with womanhood. Like the adopted child who finally locates its parents only to discover that they are loveless strangers, my inability to find a home as a mother impressed me as something not about the world but about my own unwantedness. I seemed, as a woman, to be extraneous.

And so I did two things: I reverted to my old male-inflected identity; and I conscripted my husband into care of the children. He was to take the part of that twin, femininity. He was to offer her a body of her own to shelter in, for she didn't seem able to find peace in me. My notion was that we would live together as two hybrids, each of us half male and half female. That was equality, was it not? He gave up his law job, and I gave up the exclusivity of my primitive maternal right over the children. These were our preparatory sacrifices to the new gods, whose future protection we hoped to live under. Ten years later, sitting in a solicitor's office on a noisy main road in North London, my maternalism did indeed seem primitive to me, almost barbaric. The children belong to me – this was not the kind of rudimentary phrase-making I generally went in for. Yet it was the only thought in my head, there in the chrome-and-glass office, with the petite solicitor in tailored black sitting opposite. I was thin and gaunt with distress, yet in her presence I felt enormous, rough-hewn, a maternal rock encrusted with ancient ugly emotion. She told me I had no rights of any kind. The law in these cases didn't operate on the basis of rights. What mattered was the precedent, and the precedent could be as unprecedented as you liked. So there was no primitive reality after all, it seemed. There was no such thing as a mother, a father. There was only civilisation. She told me I was obliged to support my husband financially, possibly for ever. But he's a qualified lawyer, I said. And I'm just a writer. What I meant was, he's a man. And I'm just a woman. The old voodoo still banging its drum, there in the heart of marital darkness. The solicitor raised her slender eyebrows, gave me a bitter little smile. Well, then he knew exactly what he was doing, she said.

Summer came, clanging days of glaring sunshine in the seaside town where I live, the gulls screaming in the early dawn, a glittering agitation everywhere, the water a vista of smashed light. I could no longer sleep; my consciousness filled up with the lumber of dreams, of broken-edged sections of the past heaving and stirring in the undertow. At the school gate, collecting my daughters, the other women looked somehow quaint to me, as people look when seen across a distance. I saw them as though from the annihilated emptiness of the ocean, people inhabiting land, inhabiting a construction. They had not destroyed their homes. Why had I destroyed my home? Visiting my sister, I sat in her kitchen while she folded laundry. I watched her fold her husband's shirts, his trousers. It shocked me to see these male garments, to see her touching them. She seemed to be touching something forbidden. Her right to handle these forbidden items overwhelmed me.

You know the law, my husband said over the phone. He was referring to my obligation to give him money.

I know what's right, I said.

Call yourself a feminist, he said.

What I need is a wife, jokes the stressed-out feminist career woman, and everyone laughs. The joke is that the feminist's pursuit of male values has led her to the threshold of female exploitation. This is irony. Get it? The feminist scorns that silly complicit creature, the housewife. Her first feminist act may have been to try to liberate her own housewife mother, and discover that rescue was neither wanted nor required. I hated my mother's unwaged status, her servitude, her domesticity, undoubtedly more than she herself did, for she never said she disliked them at all. Yet I stood accused of recreating exactly those conditions in my own adult life. I had hated my husband's unwaged domesticity just as much as I had hated my mother's; and he, like her, had claimed to be contented with his lot. Why had I hated it so? Because it represented dependence. But there was more to it than that, for it might be said that dependence is an agreement between two people. My father depended on my mother too: he couldn't cook a meal, or look after children from the office. They were two halves that made up a whole. What, morally speaking, is half a person? Yet the two halves were not the same: in a sense my parents were a single compartmentalised human being. My father's half was very different from my mother's, but despite the difference neither half made any sense on its own. So it was in the difference that the problem lay.

My notion of half was more like the earthworm's: you cut it in two but each half remains an earthworm, wriggling and fending for itself. I earned the money in our household, did my share of the cooking and cleaning, paid someone to look after the children while I worked, picked them up from school once they were older. And my husband helped. It was his phrase, and still is: he helped me. I was the compartmentalised modern woman, the woman having it all, and he helped me to be it, to have it. But I didn't want help: I wanted equality. In fact, this idea of help began to annoy me. Why couldn't we be the same? Why couldn't he be compartmentalised too? And why, exactly, was it helpful for a man to look after his own children, or cook the food that he himself would eat? Helpful is what a good child is to its mother. A helpful person is someone who performs duties outside their own sphere of responsibility, out of the kindness of their heart. Help is dangerous because it exists outside the human economy: the only payment for help is gratitude. And did I not have something of the same gratuitous tone where my wage-earning was concerned? Did I not think there was something awfully helpful about me, a woman, supporting my own family?

And so I felt, beneath the reconfigured surface of things, the tension of the old orthodoxies. We were a man and a woman who in our struggle for equality had simply changed clothes. We were two transvestites, a transvestite couple – well, why not? Except that I did both things, was both man and woman, while my husband – meaning well – only did one. Once, a female friend confessed to me that she admired our life but couldn't have lived it herself. She admitted the reason – that she would no longer respect her husband if he became a wife. We were, then, admirable – me for not needing a man, and him for being willing not to be one. But the admiration interested me. What, precisely, was being admired? And how could what was admirable entail the loss of respect?

Sometimes my awareness of my own competence alarmed me. How would I remain attached to the world if not by need? I didn't appear to need anyone: I could do it all myself. I could do everything. I was both halves: did that mean I was whole? In a sense I was living at the high point of feminist possibility: there was no blueprint beyond 'having it all'. The richness of that phrase, its suggestion of an unabashed splendour, was apposite. To have both motherhood and work was to have two lives instead of one, was a stunning refinement of historical female experience, and to the people who complained that having it all meant doing it all I would have said, yes, of course it does. You don't get 'all' for nothing. 'Having it all', like any form of success, requires hard work. It requires an adoption of the heroic mode of being. But the hero is solitary, individualistic, set apart from the human community. She is a wanderer, forever searching out the Holy Grail, forever questing, pursuing the goal that will provide the accurate reflection of her own abilities. The hero, being exceptional, is essentially alone.

So I was both man and woman, but over time the woman sickened, for her gratifications were fewer. I had to keep out of the way, keep out of the kitchen, keep a certain distance from my children, not only to define my husband's femininity but also to appease my own male values. The oldest trick in the sexist book is the female need for control of children. I perceived in the sentimentality and narcissism of motherhood a threat to the objectivity that as a writer I valued so highly. But it wasn't control of the children I was necessarily sickening for. It was something subtler – prestige, the prestige that is the mother's reward for the work of bearing her offspring. And that prestige was my husband's. I had given it to him or he had taken it – either way, it was what he got out of our arrangement. And the domestic work I did was in a sense at the service of that prestige, for it encompassed the menial, the trivial, the frankly boring, as though I were busily working behind the scenes to ensure the smooth running of the spectacle onstage. I wasn't male after all – men didn't do drudgery. And I wasn't female either: I felt ugly, for the things that were mine – dirty laundry, VAT returns – were not pretty at all. In fact, there was nothing pretty that gave me back a reflection of myself. I went to Paris for two days with my husband, determined while I was there to have my hair cut in a French salon. Wasn't this what women did? Well, I wanted to be womanised; I wanted someone to restore to me my lost femininity. A male hairdresser cut off all my hair, giggling as he did it, amusing himself during a dull afternoon at the salon by giving a tired blank-faced mother of two something punky and *nouvelle vague*. Afterwards, I wandered in the Paris streets, anxiously catching my reflection in shop windows. Had a transformation occurred, or a defacement? I wasn't sure. My husband wasn't sure either. It seemed terrible that between us we couldn't establish the truth. It seemed terrible, in broad daylight, in those public anonymous streets, not to know.

Sometimes, in the bath, the children cry. Their nakedness, or the warm water, or the comfort of the old routine, something, anyway, dislodges their sticking-plaster emotions and shows the wound beneath. It is my belief that I gave them that wound, so now I must take all the blame. Another version of the heroic, where the hero and the villain are hard to tell apart.

I wounded them and in this way I learned truly to love them. Or rather, I admitted it, admitted this love, admitted how much of it there was. I externalised it; internalised, it had been an instrument of self-torture. But now it was out in the world, visible, practical. What is a loving mother? It is someone whose self-interest has been displaced into her actual children. Her children's suffering causes her more pain than her own: it is Mary at the foot of the cross. In church, at the Easter service, I used to be struck by the description of Mary's emotional state, for amid that drama of physical torment, it was said that she felt as though a sword had been run through her heart. It interested me that such an image was applied to her feelings, an image that came to her from the cold hard outer world, from the physical plane of men. Somehow, in the transition from other to mother, the active becomes passive, the actual theoretical, the physical emotional, the objective subjective. The blow is softened: when my children cry a sword is run through my heart. Yet it is I who am also the cause of their crying. And for a while I am undone by this contradiction, by the difficulty of connecting the person who acted out of self-interest with the heartbroken mother who has succeeded her. It seems to be the fatal and final evolution of the compartmentalised woman, a kind of personality disorder, like schizophrenia.

Winter comes: the days are brief and pale, the sea retracted as though into unconsciousness. The coldly silvered water turns quietly on the shingle. There are long nights of stars and frost, and in the morning frozen puddles lie like little smashed mirrors in the road. We sleep many hours, like people recovering from an operation. Pain is so vivid, yet the stupor of recovery is such that pain's departure often goes unnoticed. You simply realise, one day, that it has gone, leaving a curious blank in the memory, a feeling of transitive mystery, as though the person who suffered is not – not quite – the same as the person who now walks around well. Another compartment has been created, this one for keeping odds and ends in, stray parts of experience, questions for which the answers were never found.

We rearrange the furniture to cover up the gaps. We economise, take in a lodger, get a fish tank. The fish twirl and pirouette eternally amid the fronds, regardless of what day it is. The children go to their father's and come back again. They no longer cry: they complain heartily about the inconvenience of the new arrangements. They have colour in their faces. A friend comes to stay and remarks on the sound of laughter in the house, like bird-song after the silence of winter. But it is winter still: we go to a Christmas carol service and I watch the other families. I watch mother and father and children. And I see it so clearly, as though I were looking in at them through a brightly lit window from the darkness outside; see the story in which they play their roles, their parts, with the whole world as a backdrop. We're not part of that story any more, my children and I. We belong more to the world, in all its risky disorder, its fragmentation, its freedom. The world is constantly evolving, while the family endeavours to stay the same. Updated, refurbished, modernised, but essentially the same. A house in the landscape, both shelter and prison.

We sing the carols, a band of three. I have sung these songs since my earliest recollection, sung them year after year: first as a tradition-loving child in the six-strong conventional family pew; later as a young woman who most ardently called herself a feminist; later still as a wife and mother in whose life these irreconcilable principles – the traditional and the radical, the story and the truth – had out of their hostility hatched a kind of cancer. Looking at the other families I feel our stigma, our loss of prestige: we are like a Gypsy caravan parked up among the houses, itinerant, temporary. I see that we have lost a degree of protection, of certainty. I see that I have exchanged one kind of prestige for another, one set of values for another, one scale for another. I see too that we are more open, more capable of receiving than we were; that should the world prove to be a generous and wondrous place, we will perceive its wonders.

I begin to notice, looking in through those imaginary brightly lit windows, that the people inside are looking out. I see the women, these wives and mothers, looking out. They seem happy enough, contented enough, capable enough: they are well dressed, attractive, standing with their men and their children. Yet they look around, their mouths moving. It is as though they are missing something or wondering about something. I remember it so well, what it was to be one of them. Sometimes one of these glances will pass over me and our eyes will briefly meet. And I realise she can't see me, this woman whose eyes have locked with mine. It isn't that she doesn't want to, or is trying not to. It's just that inside it's so bright and outside it's so dark, and so she can't see out, can't see anything at all.

II: A TRAGIC PASTIME

Louise Bourgeois

Suites on Fabric

The artist is a person in whom there has been no cae-
sura with the creativity of childhood: how, then, will
she herself become a mother? For the artist is a perceiver, and the mother the first and fundamental object
of perception, the first image, the Madonna of earliest Christian iconography. What will the outcome be
when these two identities – perceiver and perceived –
become one? The artist-mother has to maintain her
own links to childhood and to the sense of freedom and
irresponsibility that is the condition of her creativity.
And her actual child – will it be, in its own freedom,
her rival; in its status as her creation the rival of her art?

These are the questions an artist may ask of herself,
but to ask them of her art is to seek new, public kinds
of legitimacy for the female modes of private enquiry.
In these suites of images Louise Bourgeois explores the
interface of public and private in female experience.
Working on fabric – utilitarian, personal, domestic –
she represents that interface as both reimagined and
real. Cloth expresses the new legitimacy, soft and
unprestigious, mediating between body and world, a
record of female process. And it is through the concept
of process that the legitimacy is to be sought, for in the

organic, the evolutionary, lie the sources of woman's authority. Woman has special knowledge of process as the unifying characteristic of all that can be made: she understands it because she is subject to it, has experienced it as both curative and destructive, as health and disease, knows that its transformations are sometimes indistinguishable from deformities. *Nature Study* enquires into this organic basis of form and finds at once menace and possibility in the vegetable mechanics of growth, which beget both flowers and monsters. Who or what governs this process? What is being expressed through the mutability of nature, and from where does the expression come? In art, surely, form is immutable, so how will the artist surrender to the principle of growth that is the basis of her fleshy being? But she too can create: it need not be surrender but alliance. She can look into nature as into a mirror. The woman is shown emanating the power of form, finding its source to be her own body. Yet alliance is tense, nerve-wracking, always in danger of collapse. Sometimes she sees growth as mere profusion or extrusion, unstoppable, verging on the loss of its own meaning.

In *Self Portrait* the idea of the human form under the rule of nature causes alarm: woman has not yet asserted her alliance with the process of growth; instead, the whole concept of the self is under threat. The self begins as simple, virginal, childlike. Coupling, too, is innocent and childlike, the mutual narcissism of two distinct forms. It is creation that is ambiguous. The creative process that confirmed and organised the artist's self disrupts the mother's. Pregnant, she cannot see her creation; it is inside her; it threatens to displace her identity, her importance. Fine, then let it be ejected, expelled. Now she can see it, but her body has been left with the knowledge of pain and of its own muta- bility. In creating this new form her own form has been broken. There they stand, her works, intact, the image not of herself but of their father. And she herself is not unfixed, continually transmogrifying: she is a serpent, a spider, a sow-like field of breasts, an amputee; some- times she fuses with man or exchanges characteristics with him; sometimes she is merely one enlarged aspect of herself. But this too is a process; she emerges from it in glimpses, strong, fiercer, Medusa-haired, a kind of rayed goddess. She is less unified, more cerebral, more beautiful: an artist, after all, in the act of record- ing herself.

The Fragile offers a different, poignant vision of these same events. It is a commentary on love, deli- cate and evanescent compared with the drama of the woman artist's struggles with nature. Here the child speaks, tracing the maternal form again and again – drawing Mummy, the dextrous spider who spins and weaves. These are a child's perceptions of the primary image of its parent, yet their knowledge is the mother's knowledge too, her knowledge of her own body as an unstable form. Resolution is sought in these fused perceptions: perhaps the artist herself can, through her child, return to the childlike state of freedom and creativity. And she remains, after all, a daughter: the spider, Mummy, belongs to her too. This arachnoid maternal shape is of more than biographical interest. It bespeaks Bourgeois's familial links with the arts of weaving, but its power as a representation of maternal ambivalence is also striking. Mother is both static and busy, many-limbed but imprisoned; she is ugly and useful, frightening and familiar, so competent that a kind of helplessness adheres to her emotional and spiritual being, atop the clever busy legs. The spider is benevolent and productive, a worker, a provider, but she is fundamentally unfree. She traps things in her web; she embroiders her tiny corner of the universe.

The artistic notion of process, of growth and reproduction as vegetable forms on which the artist seeks to impose morality and meaning, is interwoven in these works with the countercurrent of memory. The process of recollection is asserted here as the foundation stone of individual identity: it is, finally, immutability, that which can't be transformed by nature. The meditative horizons of *Ode à la Bièvre*, the river beside which Bourgeois had her childhood home, are distinct in their geometric calmness and abstraction from the sometimes tormented feminine forms of *Self Portrait* and *The Fragile*, or the anarchic self-absorption of *The Cross-Eyed Woman*. Through the process of memory the artist recovers balance. She is released from her tortured body, becomes unbodied, returns to objectivity.

In the concentric circles of the final image, as though a pebble had been tossed into the river's waters, the human presence is readmitted, the relationship of self to natural form iterated once more; but quietly, peacefully, soundless and transient as the ripples that will grow fainter and eventually disappear, so that soon the surface will restore itself as though they had never been there at all.

I Am Nothing, I Am Everything

Assisi lies an hour away to the south-east. The day is overcast: clouds sag over the plain. Now and again there is a motiveless gust of wind like an outburst of temper across the flat fields that subsides as suddenly as it came. It is Sunday. The great grey drifting sky, so deep overhead and unalleviated, recalls the Sundays of my childhood with their strange double nature of privation and feasting, a character impassable and final in its duality. The week was dead: it passed away somewhere between Mass and Sunday lunch, which between them finished it off, knocked the living daylights out of it with the sacerdotal rod and the Sunday roast. There was no hope given out for Monday, or for Tuesday either. Week after week they led back to the same impasse, the same nullifying conclusion. I still have a Sunday feeling, even now; a feeling that is like a bruise or mark on the skin, that is tender when it is touched.

From far away, the Basilica di San Francesco can be seen, standing on its hill in a tent of cloud. At the front there is a buttress wall, blank and pagan-looking, frightening in its enormity. The building's long, forbidding colonnaded walkway extends from its side, like the huge dark wing of a bird of prey. I am familiar with the

giantism of Catholic architecture. At the pilgrim centre of Lourdes in France the main square and basilica
are so large that they harmonise unexpectedly with the
iconography of late capitalism, with the airport termi-
nal and the runway and the shopping mall. And indeed
both are determinedly global in their perspective: vis-
itors surrender their separateness at the sheer scale of
the enterprise, without protest. It must be imagined that
people are pleased to be relieved of their individuality,
though that doesn't seem to be the case when disaster
strikes. Then it is the impersonal they fear more than
anything else.

As we draw near, the Sunday feeling grows stronger,
the atmosphere of Catholicism more unmistakable.
There are coach parks, scores of them, for it is in the
spectacle of mass transportation that these large-scale
beliefs like to show their might. We are controlled
and directed by traffic police, by zoning, by different-
coloured signs with numbered boxes. The traffic
police wear white gloves. They point and prohibit
and occasionally permit. We wait a long time. At
last we are given a zone and a number and allowed
through. These precautions have not been put in place
to marshal admirers of the early frescoes of Giotto,
beautiful though they are reputed to be. It is St Francis who is causing the crush. All that remains of him
are the bones that lie in the basilica's cold heart, but
it is the bones the coach parties have come for. The
mania for the tangible is the predictable consequence

of the intangibility of religious belief, though it has always bewildered me that it should be among the relics of the actual that the missing link between faith and reality is sought. At the Catholic convent school I attended, the nuns were forever debating the authenticity of the Shroud of Turin, or the scrolls of Fatima, or the splinters of the true cross that were in ever-increasing circulation around the Catholic world and that put together could have made a hundred crosses. Such things roused their interest as individuals and, I suppose, alleviated the dreary impersonality of their beliefs. They were a form of attention, of love, for these women had given their lives to Jesus and had nothing whatever to show for it. Their love had no object, and in the end any bone or bit of cloth would do, just as a baby needs a blanket or a teddy bear to soothe him in his mother's absences. Once, our class was taken to see the hand of Margaret Clitherow, which the Order kept preserved in fluid at their convent in York, and those girls who screamed were immediately given detention.

I have been reading about St Francis. He was not always the poor anti-materialist who befriended the birds: he came from a family of rich Assisi cloth merchants. He was born in 1182, to doting parents who freighted him with their care and their ambition. His mother named him Giovanni, after John the Baptist, for she desired him to be a religious leader; but his father, who was away on business at the time of the birth, changed the name when he returned, furiously asserting that he did not want the child to be signed over to God. He intended him to work in the family business and drove him hard at his studies of Latin and mathematics, but no doubt he approved of his son's popularity and vigorous social appetites too, for these were suitably ungodly pastimes, and besides, ambition is gratified wherever its object finds approval in the world. Francis danced and feasted and passed his nights in riotous style with his aristocratic friends, while by day he studied and worked in his father's shop. One day a beggar came in to ask for money and Francis threw him out, but a feeling of compunction made him go after the man with a bag of coins and beg his forgiveness. Francis's father disapproved of such spiritual melodrama, and his friends ridiculed it.

Some time later Assisi declared war against neighbouring Perugia and Francis immediately enlisted. He was ambitious for knightly glory and prestige: and for escape, too, it would seem, from his parents and their conflicting desires for him. Later this need would take desperate forms, but as yet Francis perhaps believed that he could free himself by a worldly route. Almost as soon as he set off he was captured, and was imprisoned for a year. When he returned to Assisi he was ill and took to his bed. There a change took place. It expressed itself in a need to give away his own possessions, a form of behaviour that was also the deepest challenge he could offer to his father's authority.

Francis began to spend his days alone, forlornly wandering in the countryside around the town. One day he came across a small church that lay in ruins and believed that he heard a voice telling him to repair it. More precisely, the voice is said to have ordered him to 'repair my house which has fallen into ruin'. Another man might have acted on this injunction in the grand manner for which it appears to legislate, but Francis responded by selling some of his father's cloth without permission and beginning restoration work on the little church with the proceeds. It is rare for the voice of God to initiate a direct attack on the property of the human father. It is as though Francis's God were a projection of himself, a kind of universal victim ravaged by the world's misunderstanding and neglect. Perhaps his spirit had been crushed after all, for like a child his sympathies ever after lay with dumb creatures, with the birds and bees whose patron saint he became. His father, Pietro, accused Francis of theft and led him before the bishop. Pietro explained the whole case, the wealth and education from which his son had profited, the ingratitude his increasingly strange behaviour evinced and the crime in which it had culminated, a crime the more outrageous for being perpetrated against his own father, to whom he owed everything, down to the clothes on his back. At this, Francis committed his final act of rejection: in front of the bishop he removed all of his clothes and gave them back to his father. What lengths he went to, both to goad and to free himself from his oppressive parent! To hand back your own clothes is the prelude to immolation itself, to the giving back of the body that has struggled to be free and failed. And Francis did go on to lead a life of great privation and denial, in which his interest in his new father and patriarch – God – seems to have been more than a little abstracted. His was a pure brand of nihilism that sought only to shield its most abject and defenceless victims from the evil of humankind. At the end of his life he instructed his followers to bury him at a place called Hell's Hill, a bleak tract of land where executions were customarily held. His sufferings from tuberculosis were extreme, and it was during this final illness that he wrote the 'Canticle of the Creatures', a love poem to the unpopulated earth, to the sun and wind and water, to a dumb and beautiful Mother Nature whom he idolised for her impartiality, her lack of motive, her generosity that did not enslave, her abundance that was without cause or consequence.

Two years after Francis's death in 1226, the cult of his celebrity was born. He was canonised, and the Pope laid the foundation stone for the basilica on his grave. He who had suffered so bitterly from the tyranny of identity, whose psyche found relief only in the dissolution of ownership and the casting off of material things, whose eyes dwelt for consolation on what was small and beneath notice, was to be pinioned for ever beneath the weight of a giant edifice of unparalleled splendour, in a place he had chosen for its lack of prestige, but which was henceforth to invoke the very origins of human aspiration itself and bear the name of Paradise Hill.

Reading Vasari's *Lives of the Artists*, one begins to notice a minor consistency of an unexpected sort. The artists of the Renaissance, almost without exception, profited early in life from their fathers' help in the recognition and exercise of their talents. Michelangelo, it is true, was occasionally beaten for spending his time drawing when he should have been studying, but by the time he was fourteen his father had changed his tune and apprenticed him at a living wage to the painter Ghirlandaio. But it is mostly the case that the child-artist, who in other eras was grudgingly received as a delinquent or an idiot, was in this time and place favoured and forwarded, soldered to the world by the paternalistic hand. And perhaps the psychic health of the art of the Renaissance, its confidence and sociability and insatiable love of humankind, issues from this prosaic and fundamental source.

Cimabue, born in 1240, whose works adorn the Basilica of St Francis, is credited by Vasari with being the artist who initiated the great restoration of the art of painting in Italy. At school he would cover his books with drawings instead of reading them: his parents congratulated him on his originality. When a group of Greek craftsmen was brought to Florence to decorate the Gondi Chapel in Santa Maria Novella, Cimabue truanted school altogether and spent whole days watching them work. His father approached these craftsmen and elicited their agreement to take Cimabue on as an apprentice, for according to Vasari he had a great respect for his son and believed that his inclinations ought to be trusted. How different from poor St Francis, who only had to show an inclination for his father to move to crush it! And how different the pursuit of truth that followed, the one so punitive and painful and the other so vigorous and beautiful. Cimabue quickly became famous, so famous that when he painted a large new Madonna for Santa Maria Novella the painting was processed through the streets to the sound of trumpets and a cheering crowd. One day, he was walking in the countryside when he came across a young shepherd boy sitting in a field, drawing one of his own sheep with a pointed stone on a smooth piece of rock. This was Giotto. Cimabue was so astonished by his talent that he asked the boy to come and live with him, and the boy replied that if his father agreed, then he would. The father was delighted, and Giotto went back with Cimabue to Florence, where, as Vasari admits, he rapidly diminished Cimabue's glory by becoming one of the greatest painters the world has ever known. Dante summed up the situation in *The Divine Comedy*:

> Once, Cimabue thought to hold the field
> In painting; Giotto's all the rage today;
> The other's fame lies in the dust concealed.

It was in the Basilica di San Francesco that these first artists of the Renaissance evolved their artistic vision, for the edifice quickly grew so large that a certain blankness adhered to it, and adheres to it still. It is easy to enlarge the scale of a human construction: what is hard is to amplify its brain. The basilica was a dinosaur that needed to be rendered articulate. That was what the artists were for, to fill in its blankness, to program it with meaning and significance. The modest spirit of St Francis alone could not fill its barn-like spaces: it required the seasoning of art to flavour the bland atmosphere of pilgrimage.

Yet the modern-day pilgrims like their blandness, their plain fare. The basilica is full of them, passing the painted walls with barely a glance. The specifics of art are too strong for their palates. It is bones they have come for in their air-conditioned coaches; bones, and the experience of their own coming, their massing: the basic unit of life, entire unto itself, moving and massing together like polyps on the ocean bed. Held as they are in the unblinking stare of existence, interpretation and art do not concern them. The painted walls of the basilica are no more to them than the texture of the rock on which their colony has massed itself. Those walls are now faded and damaged with time: they have their own fame, their own divinity, but the pilgrims dislike people looking at paintings. They hiss and shush and send over angry stares. Now and then a message is broadcast over the sound system, reminding those who are not in the basilica to attend Mass that absolute silence is required or they will be asked to leave. Then the voice of the priest singing the liturgy issues from the crackling speakers once more, a sound that is both automatic and animal, like the loud call of some primitive creature whose interminable cadences now and again invite the unanimous caterwauling of his neighbours.

In the upper basilica there are a large number of frescoes depicting the life of St Francis. Until recently it was believed that Giotto had painted them, but my researches have informed me that it is now known that he did not. Nevertheless, his name remains there, in an engraved perspex rectangle on the basilica wall. Elsewhere in the basilica there are works by Cimabue, Simone Martini, Lorenzetti and the real Giotto, and none of them are labelled at all. They are difficult to find: they lie in sepulchral darkness among the vaults of the lower church, like prisoners in a dungeon. The customary modern appurtenances of the art lover are nowhere to be found. There are no lights, no silken tasselled ropes, no information. One is obstructed and put off the scent at every opportunity. The broadcast warnings intensify: the shushing and the hostile stares come thick and fast through the gloom, for it is in the lower church that the bones lie, and the closer we get to them the more vigorously art is derided.

I begin to feel a little outraged. It is they who seem heretical to me, these spiritual bureaucrats with their rules and regulations, their monotonous chanting, their punitive demeanour and their threats of expulsion. It is they who are insolent: so quick to damn and shame, and glorying so in the execution of it. As a child I was accustomed to the way adults seized on Christianity as a tool, a moralising weapon they had fashioned in their own subconscious: when they unsheathed it I would glimpse the strange, dark chasm of repression and subjectivity, a place that seemed like a crack in the safe surface of the world; and it did appear to me that judgement lay down there, flowing like a black river within the tributaries of personalities, from a nameless common source. But now I found the Christian story all human, like literature: it was a long time since it had been raised as a weapon over my head. It is perhaps for exactly this reason that the pilgrims object to the Giotto-lovers. The whole place, I now see, has set itself against art as against a rival religion. A group of teenagers with clipboards murmur in front of Lorenzetti's *Madonna dei Tramonti* and are instantly shot down with a volley of glares like a firing squad's fusillade. A child asks a question of its parent concerning Giotto's *Flight into Egypt* and is bludgeoned from all sides with disapproval. They are enraged, these people queuing to worship at the strange, sealed hexagonal tomb. Like Jesus, Francis was a misfit who has become an orthodoxy. But the Pharisee, it seems, was well drawn as an eternal human type. Of what, precisely, are we meant to feel ashamed? Is their faith so fragile, so impacted, that the whole world must be silent while it is teased out? They seem to disapprove so instinctively, as a hand gropes in the darkness for a switch. A little light comes on in their eyes: it reveals something, a sacred space in the brain that perhaps otherwise they would have had trouble finding their way to, with a bone lying in it on a little heap of dust.

In the right wing of the transept there is a famous painting of St Francis by Cimabue. He is small, hunched, unsmiling. He wears a monk's tonsure and brown cassock and clutches a Bible in his hands. His eyes are large, almond-shaped, heavy-lidded, of a light-brown colour: their expression is unutterably sad. It is not the sadness that shows in the rolling whites of a saint's upturned, imploring gaze. It is a sadness that you see in the eyes of people who were unhappy children. His soft, full mouth trembles like a ripple in the surface of water. It is curious to see the paths of St Francis and Cimabue cross in this shadowy corner of the basilica. Cimabue painted a large number of frescoes in the upper and lower church alike, virtually none of which survive. He was reputed to be arrogant and perfectionistic, rejecting work that bore the slightest flaw in conception or technique. This was a new personality in the thirteenth-century world, this temperamental individualist. In those days a painter was a craftsman: the artist did not yet exist. The craftsman did not throw away work because it was less than perfect. He was the master of his materials, but he was not yet their author.

Cimabue couldn't have cared less what his materials were worth, that much is clear. He could see something beyond himself and he made a path to it out of art. It was he who had to do it, for only he knew where his vision lay. And it had to be right, flawless, for what is the good of a path that doesn't lead where it is meant to? In the painting of St Francis, the saint says, 'I am nothing'; the artist says, 'I am everything.' Cimabue reinvented painting by reinventing the artist as visionary, as individualist, as risk-taker, as criminal and hero. And he restored to the painted human form its softness and mortality, its animal nature and the grandeur of its emotion. This was the old knowledge of the classical world, which the Christian story froze into a thousand-year hibernation. Now it was to be reborn as something new. Humanity had insisted that a link be forged between gods and mortals, but it was a long time before this new situation could be described: there were many rigid Madonnas to be painted, many stiff and gilded Annunciations, many primitive Nativities and stark Crucifixions before the connection could be made. Now the artist-individual could paint the subject-individual, the creature who contains everything – good and evil, truth and illusion, life and death – within himself. Now, at last, he could begin to capture reality.

There is a painting in the lower church by the unknown 'Maestro di San Francesco' of St Francis preaching to the

birds. In its own way it is a masterpiece of characterisation, according the Franciscan vision the full measure of
its eccentricity. It is as tragicomic as its subject, for what
could better illustrate the analgesic nature of insanity
than the belief that one is understood by birds? Virginia
Woolf, in her bouts of madness, experienced this delusion, and there is a photograph by Cartier-Bresson
of the painter Matisse in old age, sitting in a room full of
empty birdcages. White doves have roosted on top of
their open prison: Matisse holds one in his hands. He
appears to be addressing it, for like Francis he cleaved
to what was innocent and childlike, to the positivism
of dumb nature. 'I have always tried to hide my own
efforts,' he wrote, 'and wished my works to have the
lightness and joyousness of a springtime which never
lets anyone suspect the labours it has cost.'

Francis preaches to the birds and the birds listen
respectfully, lined up in neat rows on the grass. Their
little heads are attentive: their eyes are bright. Like children they look up, for Francis is much taller than they.
Their tiny beaks are lifted and their wings are folded
at their sides. And Francis, in his cassock, speaks on, a
tutelary finger raised, like a gentle lunatic in a public
park. Upstairs there is a frescoed image of the moment
he returned his clothes to his father in front of the
bishop. It occurs to me that it is not for his godliness
alone that the pilgrims come to worship Francis. His
story, born as it is out of human psychology, is emblem-
atic of the same consciousness that was simultaneously

struggling to express itself in art. I am nothing; I am everything. Perhaps, after all, the pilgrims shush and glare at us for the same reason that we roll our eyes at them. It is the rise of the personal we are reverencing, in its different forms. It is meaning we have come for, of one sort or another. But most of all it is sympathy, sympathy that we want and must have, only sympathy, from bones or from paint.

We go out into the grey, heavy afternoon. The basilica stands at the foot of the town, on a jutting peninsula of land where the earth falls away to all sides. Below it lies the plain, sinking into its own flat eternity like a separate element, so that from above there is the feeling of terminus, of the sea seen from the last cliffs that are the boundary of the habitable world. We walk away from it, up into the cobbled streets that twist and turn uphill. A small, hard rain begins to fall, dashed down in handfuls. Every now and then a monk passes by, impervious to the water. They wear immaculate cassocks and sandals with belts of rope swinging at their waists; they beam at everyone they see. They look like extras on a film set, walking the antique streets beneath the artificial rain in their unblemished costumes. We have lunch in a restaurant, gnocchi made by a chef who stands only a few feet away behind his little hatch and beams at us too while we eat. The children want to buy a souvenir. We stand in a shop and look at nightlights made of moulded plastic, which show the Virgin encased in a plastic grotto that lights up pink when it is switched on. There are T-shirts and table mats and baseball caps, aprons and napkin rings and plastic pens, figurines and frisbees and extravagant embroidered wall hangings, all bearing an image of St Francis of Assisi. It is not Cimabue's image: it is a computerised logo, a brand. There are expensive porcelain statues, too, about ten inches high, that depict him among the animals: birds have alighted on his hands, a deer rests at his feet, a lamb lies across his shoulders. The statues are entirely white: his monkish garment looks like a Grecian robe, falling in long milk-white folds to his feet.

I myself had exactly this statue as a child. I was given it on the occasion of my First Communion. It seems strange to me that they should still be producing it, all this time later, so closely did I identify it with a phase of my own life. For years it stood on the mantelpiece of my bedroom, along with a blue china plaque bearing a relief of the Virgin Mary in a wreath of china flowers. The plaque is also for sale in the souvenir shop in Assisi. After I had left home these things remained in my room in my parents' house, but then several years ago my mother gave them back to me: I was grown up, and had a house of my own to put them in. I didn't want them, for I never felt that they were actually mine, and their presence in this shop seems to prove it. There was something unsavoury about them, something threatening: a sterility or morbidity, like the funerary displays in an undertaker's window. There they had stood on my childhood mantelpiece and though I never really looked at them their purity was dreadful and frightening to me, for it was clear that these were children's ornaments and when I glimpsed them out of the corner of my eye I saw children's graves. This was how the pill of religion was always forced down, with flavours too bitter and too sweet to mask one another. But I took the statue and the plaque back anyway, feeling that I should. When I opened the box again, all those years later, that flavour rose out in all its potency. I remembered how deeply the feeling of sterility had impressed itself on me, the feeling of Sunday, of nuns in their habits, of old bones, of disapproval and shame and of everything that could have no further issue, no continuance, in this world or the next. It all seemed to be paving the way not to heaven, nor even to hell, but to absolute and final nothingness.

Later still I found the statue again and put it in my children's bedroom. I don't know why I did: again, I only felt that I should. It looked anomalous and out of place, next to the little glass dolphin from Venice, the shell collection, the glass dome that you shook to make the snow whirl over the miniature Manhattan skyline. But one day I was in their room and I knocked it over by accident and broke it. I put the broken pieces in a shoebox, and hid them at the back of a cupboard.

Shakespeare's Sisters

Can we, in the twenty-first century, identify something that could be called 'women's writing'? To be sure, women are sometimes to be found receiving the winner's cheque for the Man Booker or Costa prizes, just as they are sometimes to be found piloting your flight home from New York. It may be that in both cases certain sectors of society do not feel entirely secure. But it seems to me that 'women's writing' by nature would not seek equivalence in the male world. It would be a writing that sought to express a distinction, not deny it.

When a woman in the twenty-first century sits down to write, she perhaps feels rather sexless. She is inclined neither to express nor deny: she'd rather be left alone to get on with it. She might even nurture a certain hostility towards the concept of 'women's writing'. Why should she be politicised when she doesn't feel politicised? It may even, with her, be a point of honour to keep those politics as far from her prose as it is possible to get them. What compromises women – babies, domesticity, mediocrity – compromises writing even more. She is on the right side of that compromise – just. Her own life is one of freedom and entitlement, though her mother's was probably not. Yet she herself is not a man. She is a woman: it is history that has brought about this difference between herself and her mother. She can look around her and see that while women's lives have altered in some respects, in others they have remained much the same. She can look at her own body: if a woman's body signifies anything, it is that repetition is more powerful than change. But change is more wondrous, more enjoyable. It is pleasanter to write the book of change than the book of repetition. In the book of change one is free to consider absolutely anything, except that which is eternal and unvarying. 'Women's writing' might be another name for the book of repetition.

Two books – Simone de Beauvoir's *The Second Sex* and Virginia Woolf's *A Room of One's Own* – bring these thoughts to mind. Between them they shaped the discourse of twentieth-century women's writing, a shape that is still recognisable today; both, famously, are formulated around the concept of property. De Beauvoir's thesis of the great displacement of woman in history by the male initiative of ownership is the magnification of Woolf's more literary synthesis of actual and expressive female poverty. A woman needs a room of her own to be able to write; thus her silence has been the silence of dispossession. Yet there is something still deeper and more mysterious in her silence, the mystery of her actual identity. Woolf and De Beauvoir agree that a woman – even a woman with her own room – could never have written *Moby-Dick* or

War and Peace, for 'civilisation as a whole elaborates this intermediary product between the male and the eunuch that is called feminine'; and as well as lacking a room, woman has lacked a literature of her own. Half silence, half enigma: the words 'women's writing' connote not simply a literature made by women but one that arises out of, and is shaped by, a set of specifically female conditions. A book is not an example of 'women's writing' simply because it is written by a woman. Writing may become 'women's writing' when it could not have been written by a man.

De Beauvoir's woman is a beggar – she becomes one, to paraphrase, rather than is born one – comprehensively debased in her slavery, debasing herself, fawning for scraps from the male table. Woolf's woman is more in the way of a victim, a prisoner. She is actively disbarred; if her nature is warped, it is by fault of circumstance. 'Art, literature and philosophy are attempts to found the world anew on a human freedom,' writes De Beauvoir, 'that of the creator. To foster such an aim, one must first unequivocally posit oneself as a freedom.' A woman can be given freedom, certainly, but she can never have always had it: 'one must first emerge within [the world] in sovereign solitude if one wants to try to grasp it anew.' The temptation for the woman writer, De Beauvoir says, is to use writing as an escape. The woman writer wishes to avoid confrontation, for 'her great concern is to please; and as a woman she is already afraid of displeasing just because she writes . . .

The writer who is original . . . is always scandalous; what is new disturbs and antagonises; [but] women are still astonished and flattered to be accepted in the world of thinking and art, a masculine world. The woman watches her manners; she does not dare to irritate, explore, explode.'

A woman writer, then, loses her integrity – and her chance of greatness – in the attempt to join male literary culture. For, as De Beauvoir says, 'man is a sexed human being: woman is a complete individual, and equal to the male, only if she too is a sexed human being. Renouncing her femininity means renouncing part of her humanity.' Thus equality can only be arrived at by the route of difference: but what does this mean for the woman writer? Must she experience kinship with silence and enigma, as the male writer feels kinship for Moby-Dick? Twenty-first-century female culture barely acknowledges its debt to feminism: why should it? And perhaps consequently, today's woman writer is careful not to show any special interest in today's woman. Yet if black writers cease to write about what it is to be black, we do not conclude that blackness no longer has any special features, or that racism no longer exists. Oppression, being a type of relationship, can never be resolved, only reconfigured; in its ever-alternating phases of shame and receptivity, the possibility of its return must always remain. Sometimes society is receptive to the language of oppression; at other times it is not, and oppression becomes a cause of shame. Women, then, might cease to produce 'women's writing' not because they are freer but because they are more ashamed, less certain of a general receptiveness, and even, perhaps, because they suspect they might be vilified.

It is easier to be a historian than a prophet, and when Virginia Woolf said that a woman needed a room of her own and money of her own to write fiction she appeared to be alluding to a female future where possession – property – equalled words as inevitably as dispossession, in the past, had equalled silence. A woman with a room and money will be free to write – but to write what? In *A Room of One's Own* Woolf asserts two things: first, that the world – and hence its representations in art – is demonstrably male; and second, that a woman cannot create art out of a male reality. Literature, for most of its history, was a male reality. The form and structure of the novel, the perceptual framework, the very size and character of the literary sentence: these were tools shaped by men for their own uses. The woman of the future, Woolf says, will devise her own kind of sentence, her own form, and she'll use it to write about her own reality. What's more, that reality will have its own values: 'And since a novel has this correspondence to real life, its values are to some extent those of real life. But it is obvious that the values of women differ very often from the values which have been made by the other sex; naturally, this is so. Yet it is the masculine values that prevail . . . This is an important book, the critic assumes, because it deals with war. This is an insignificant book because it deals with the feelings of women in a drawing-room. A scene in a battle-field is more important than a scene in a shop – everywhere and much more subtly the difference of value persists.'

The independent woman writer, Woolf believed, would in overturning those values write what had not yet been written. The story of woman would 'light a torch in that vast chamber where nobody has yet been. It is all half lights and profound shadows like those serpentine caves where one goes with a candle peering up and down, not knowing where one is stepping.'

The future, of course, never comes: it is merely a projection from the present of the present's frustrations. In the eighty years since Woolf published *A Room of One's Own*, aspects of female experience have been elaborated on with commendable candour, as often as not by male writers. A book about war is still judged more important than a book about 'the feelings of women'. Most significantly, when a woman writes a book about war she is lauded: she has eschewed the vast unlit chamber and the serpentine caves; there is the sense that she has made proper use of her room and her money, her new rights of property. The woman writer who confines herself to her female 'reality' is by the same token often criticised. She appears to have squandered her room, her money. It is as though she has been swindled, or swindled herself; she is the victim of her own exploitation. And as for 'female values', who could say what they are? If, as Woolf claims, the values of literature are at any given moment the reflection of the values of life, then we are living in an era in which the female is once more devalued and the male pre-eminent.

Recently, reading Chekhov's *Three Sisters*, it struck me that the question of female self-expression – let's call it 'women's writing' – becomes confused precisely where the attempt is made to concretise it. Chekhov's play is based on aspects of the lives of the Brontë sisters; the three women, Olga, Irina and Masha, suffer not only from the confinement and tedium of provincial life but from something antithetical in their relationship to reality. What they feel is not embodied by what they are. They look back to childhood as a time of Edenic simplicity and happiness – as children they did not recognise gender as destiny and limitation – but now all their hopes for accomplishment, for 'becoming', have transferred themselves to their brother Andrey. The sisters ponder marriage, love, motherhood, paid work, and yet can find no answer in any of them. It isn't just female powerlessness that causes the difficulty: it is something more, a force that bears a special hostility to the actual. There is nothing they can be or become that will discharge it. This force might be called creativity; what is interesting is Chekhov's decision to omit writing from his representation of the situation, and indeed he is careful to maintain only the lightest connection in the play with the extremity of the Brontës' world. Both

the suffering and the writing are transposed into something less tangible and more generalised, something
that touches on the nature of woman herself.

Woman is filled with visions and yearnings that are
never matched by reality; she has a power of visuali-
sation, of imagination, that her lack of worldly power
forever frustrates. Yes, she might produce literature out
of this conflict in her being. But she is more likely to
produce silence. And in Chekhov's version, the conflict between being and becoming grows more severe
as life advances, because the space for intangibility
shrinks. Irina and Olga are made to share a room
because their sister-in-law wants Irina's room for her
new baby. Thus the woman who has embraced what
Woolf calls the 'masculine values', who agrees to exist
as woman on male terms, gains a territorial advantage
over the woman who has not. Moreover, the two types
of woman have become mutually hostile. The woman
who has her being in marriage and motherhood has
become part of antithetical reality, revoking property
from the woman who remains in a condition of intangible femininity.

It may be, then, that the room of one's own does not
have quite the straightforward relationship to female
creativity that Woolf imagined. She, after all, had by
dint of circumstance always had a room and money of
her own, and perhaps being the eternal conditions of
her own writing they seemed to her indispensable. Yet
she admits that the two female writers she unequivo-

cally admired – Jane Austen and Emily Brontë – wrote in shared domestic space. The room, or the lack of it, doesn't necessarily have anything to do with writing at all. It could be said that every woman should have a room of her own. But it may equally be the case that a room of her own enables the woman writer to shed her links with femininity and commit herself to the reiteration of 'masculine values'. The room itself may be the embodiment of those values, a conception of 'property' that is at base unrelated to female nature.

Woolf confesses that she does not know what women are: they have left so little trace behind them, she says, have observed such a profound silence over the centuries that they are virtually unhistoried. The woman artist must grasp the scanty threads of her forebears – Austen, George Eliot, the Brontës. She must cling on to what representation there is. Yet Chekhov is perhaps the more perceptive on this point. The representation inspired him to consider the silence, not the other way around. It is the silence itself which interests him, and it interests him not as an absence but as a presence. Woolf, in *A Room of One's Own*, sees that presence in terms of Shakespeare's imaginary sister Judith: a person she describes as being like her brother William in every respect except that of sex, who is frustrated and silenced and abused at every turn where he is recognised and advanced and congratulated. But Chekhov does not consider the female in terms of the male. He sees her as thwarted in her own being, as fundamentally unknown even to herself. In

Three Sisters, Irina expresses this concept of silence as arising from a lack of connection between emotion and actuality: 'Oh, I used to think so much of love,' she says. 'I have been thinking about it for so long by day and by night, but my soul is like a costly piano which is locked and the key lost.' She does not say who locked the piano, nor who lost the key; just that it was costly, and is silent.

Doris Lessing enlarges on these themes in her story 'To Room Nineteen', where a conventionally – if not happily – married mother of four children begins to experience the desire to have a room of her own. The desire is a kind of plague: she doesn't know why she wants the room, nor what she will use it for. But she has to have it. She does feel a strong urge to free herself from the impingement of other people: this is the only explanation she can offer, that she wants to be where no one can get at her. First she designates an unused room in the family home as 'hers', but this doesn't satisfy her. People can still find her there; the children come in and leave their toys on the floor. But more than that, she doesn't actually want to be in this room. It becomes clear that what she wants is to sever her ties with existence itself. She rents a room in a seedy hotel in an unpleasant part of town, and every afternoon she goes there and lies on the bed. This room, room number 19, she identifies as 'hers': she is upset when she arrives one afternoon to discover that it isn't free (it's a hotel, after all). To explain her disappearances, she tells her husband she is having an affair. He is pleased: he himself has affairs, and now he feels exonerated. One afternoon, in room 19, she kills herself.

In Lessing's story, as in *Three Sisters*, writing is 'silent'. We know that Lessing, a woman, wrote it, as we know that the Brontës wrote. But in both cases, the self-expressive space of the actual drama remains unfilled: Lessing's character does not go to room 19 to write bestselling novels, any more than Olga and Irina channel their frustrations into the production of literary works. Writing, 'women's writing', thus comes to mean something else, something new: it describes what it is not, it defines its opposite, silence; it puts itself at the service of what negates it. In Lessing's story the room – the room of one's own – is death, death of female reality, death as an alternative to compromise. The author acknowledges that her writing is the kin of death and silence, that her 'room' is a place menaced by compromise. And better death than the furtherance of 'masculine values'.

Woolf concedes that the woman writer might have to break everything – the sentence, the sequence, the novel form itself – to create her own literature. And she wonders, too, whether a situational link between women's lives and their work, far from impeding their writing, might actually be necessary to it; whether, in other words, it was because Austen wrote behind the door in the shared sitting room that *Pride and Prejudice* is the flawless novel it is. It is a requirement of art that the artist be unified with his or her own material.

Stumblingly, Woolf hazards the guess that a 'female' literature will be shorter, more fragmentary, interrupted, 'for interruptions there will always be'. And her own *Mrs Dalloway* might be read as a novel about its author's fear of her own ordinariness and triviality, her dread sexual ancestry with its silence and compromise and mediocrity, the awful frailty of her expressive gift, without which, as she wrote in her diary, she believed she would be nothing at all.

It may be that today's woman writer doesn't have much to do with the concept of 'women's writing'. Feminism as a cultural and political crisis comes and goes. Marriage, motherhood and domesticity are regarded as so many choices, about which there is a limited entitlement to complain. If a woman feels suffocated and grounded and bewildered by her womanhood, she feels these things alone, as an individual: there is currently no public unity among women, because since the peak of feminism the task of woman has been to assimilate herself with man. She is, therefore, occluded, scattered, disguised. Were a woman writer to address her sex, she would not know who or what she was addressing. Superficially this situation resembles equality, except that it occurs within the domination of 'masculine values'. What today's woman has gained in personal freedom she has lost in political caste. Hers is still the second sex, but she has earned the right to dissociate herself from it.

In this context Simone de Beauvoir's assertion that one is not born a woman but becomes one gains a new kind of potency. If modern woman has no identity, her 'becoming' is both more random and more mysterious. The danger, surely, is that she will 'become' – violently – in those parts of life where her sex can be experienced as unitary. In other words, if the difference of gender goes unexamined – is made to seem as though it doesn't exist – the girl will be more, not less, magnetised and fascinated by that difference. And she will look around her and see that the politicians, the captains of industry, the bankers and the power brokers and the commentators are mostly men. This may be the reason – if there can be a reason – for the woman writer to risk taking female-ness and female values as her subject. 'The fact is that the traditional woman is a mystified consciousness and an instrument of mystification,' De Beauvoir writes. 'She tries to conceal her dependence from herself, which is a way of consenting to it.' Some of the most passionate writing in *The Second Sex* concerns the ways in which women seek to protect their privileges and property under patriarchy by condemning or ridiculing the honesty of other women. This remains true today: woman continues to act as an 'instrument of mystification' precisely where she fears and denies her own dependence. For the woman writer this is a scarifying prospect. She can find herself disowned in the very act of invoking the deepest roots of shared experience. Having taken the trouble to write honestly, she can find herself being read dishonestly. And in my own experience as a writer, it is in the places where honesty is most required – because it is here that compromise and false consciousness and 'mystification' continue to endanger the integrity of a woman's life – that it is most vehemently rejected. I am talking, of course, about the book of repetition, about fiction that concerns itself with what is eternal and unvarying, with domesticity and motherhood and family life. The sheer intolerance, in the twenty-first century, for these subjects is the unarguable proof that woman is on the verge of surrendering important aspects of her modern identity.

So the woman writer looking for work will still find plenty in the task of demystification, of breaking the silence that forms like fog around iterative female experience. She won't win the Man Booker Prize for writing the book of repetition: she will, as De Beauvoir perceived, irritate and antagonise rather than please. What's worse, she may have to give back some of her privileges to write it. She may have to come out of her room, and take up her old place behind the sitting room door.

How to Get There

In F. Scott Fitzgerald's novel *The Beautiful and Damned*, the writer Dick Caramel tells of a conversation with his uncle from Kansas: 'All the old man does is tell me he just met the most wonderful character for a novel. Then he tells me about some idiotic friend of his and then he says: "There's a character for you! Why don't you write him up? Everybody'd be interested in him." Or else he tells me about Japan or Paris, or some other very obvious place, and says: "Why don't you write a story about that place? That'd be a wonderful setting for a story!"'

Anyone who has ever claimed to be a novelist will recognise this exchange. What other grown-up gets told how to do their job so often as a writer? Or rather, what is it about writing that makes other people think they know how to do it? Dick Caramel's first novel, *The Demon Lover*, goes on to become a wild publishing success, and as a consequence Caramel turns into an intolerably self-aggrandising bore. He talks constantly about money and his 'career', sounding more like a businessman than an artist, then is demolished whenever he meets someone who hasn't heard of him and his book. Fitzgerald's portrait of 'the writer' is as riddling a piece of characterisation as any he ever wrote, empathetic and damning and so ambivalent as to be cruel, almost, to himself.

Fitzgerald, like many writers of his time, went to Hollywood in search of a salaried profession: his friend Billy Wilder likened him to 'a great sculptor hired to do a plumbing job'. Commentators have expressed surprise at how hard-working and conscientious he was as a studio employee, as though something other than hard work and conscientiousness had produced *Tender is the Night* and *The Great Gatsby*. But no amount of toil could disguise the fact that Fitzgerald was no screenwriter. 'He didn't know how to connect the pipes so that the water could flow,' Wilder added. It is a memorable image, and one that evokes the vulnerability of artistic self-esteem. Those writers who flocked to Hollywood to trade in their one bankable asset, writing, might have come away with the disquieting impression that they were no good at it either.

Today's novelist has what would seem to be a more humane alternative to being a (failed) hack. The ascent of creative writing courses has given writers a different kind of work to do, and is transforming every established role – writer, reader, editor, critic – in the literary drama. Dick Caramel's conversation with his uncle is no longer a stock scene: the writer has become a 'professional' with a tenured academic status, a certified technician of language; one would ask him for advice, as one would a doctor, rather than tell him how to do his job. The terrain has become formalised, mapped out, institutionalised. People are paying to have their views about characterisation, setting, theme attended to: if you want a writer to listen to you, you'll have to sign up for an MFA.

In one way it's high time writing was formalised: academic institutions offer a shelter for literary values, and for those who wish to practise them, in a way that publishing, being increasingly market-driven, does not. Painters and musicians have long been protected in a similar way – it is both an entitlement and a necessity for creative people to study and refine their craft. Yet creative writing courses are often seen as being somehow bogus, as even threatening those literary principles they set out to enshrine, though the truth is that the separation of literary from popular values in writing has been virtually impossible to bring about. This is a source of great dynamism in literary culture, for anyone can be a writer – at the very least, while the average person believes they could not compose a symphony, a significant minority want to write a novel. There is a demand, among people with little or no track record of writing, to study the art of fiction, and while this might not give creative writing much of an academic profile, it is absolutely reflective of the way the literary world works.

A creative writing workshop will contain students whose ambitions and abilities, whose conceptions of literature itself, are so diverse that what they have in common – the desire to write – could almost be considered meaningless. Moreover, different creative

writing tutors will respond to the work presented to
them in unpredictable ways. One will like what another dislikes; contradictory advice can be given in two
different classes about the same piece of work. So the
question is, how can academic appraisal proceed on
such terms?

The upper benchmark of academic assessment is that
the work should be 'of publishable standard', which
implies (though doesn't actually state) a touching faith
in publication as an assurance of quality. Students are
asked to demonstrate a critical and theoretical understanding of their own processes; they are formally
entitled to individual attention from tutors, by rota in
workshops and by a stated number of contact hours
outside workshops; their work is regularly marked,
double-marked and submitted to an external examiner
as a fail-safe mechanism; marks are lost for misuses of,
among other things, grammar, punctuation and spell-
ing; tutors are answerable for the marks they give before
a board. Appraisal, in other words, is rather more rigorous than a lot of what happens at an editor's desk.

How are standards – publishable or otherwise –
defined? The answer is: by agreement. There is no
autocratic way of assessing literature: the shared basis
of language forbids it. Agreement is the flawed, frightening, but ultimately trustworthy process by which
writing is and always has been judged. When Virginia
Woolf read *Ulysses* she dismissed it out of hand; then
she talked about it to Katherine Mansfield and changed

her mind. Creative writing teaching is predicated on something like that model.

Language is not only the medium through which existence is transacted, it constitutes our central experiences of social and moral content, of such concepts as freedom and truth, and, most importantly, of individuality and the self; it is also a system of lies, evasions, propaganda, misrepresentation and conformity. Very often a desire to write is a desire to live more honestly through language; the student feels the need to assert a 'true' self through the language system, perhaps for the reason that this same system, so intrinsic to every social and personal network, has given rise to a 'false' self.

A piece of music or a work of art might echo to the sense of a 'true' self, but it is often through language that an adult seeks self-activation, origination, for the reason that language is the medium, the brokering mechanism, of self. The notion of 'finding your voice', simplistic as it may sound, is a therapeutic necessity, and for many people a matter of real urgency. It is also – or ought to be – a social goal. If the expansion of creative writing courses signifies anything, it isn't the cynicism of universities or the self-deception of would-be students: it means, simply, that our manner of life is dishonest, that it offers too few opportunities for self-expression, and that, for some people, there is too great a disjuncture between how things seem and how they actually feel.

A writer may be someone who has never lost their

voice, or has always had it; for a number of reasons, they have withheld themselves from immersion in the social contract. Some creative writing students are already writers, but often they are people whose immersion, conversely, has been complete: they are writers who have never actually written anything. One thing it profits a writer to learn, through teaching, is how fundamental a distinction this is.

Many people come to study creative writing out of a need the writer has wholly internalised. The writer's authority, in a sense, rests on that fact. If the democratic basis of language is what underpins the idea of the 'writers' workshop', then in that setting the writer is a free individual, enabling others to process varying degrees of confinement: confinement in artificial ideas about writing, sure enough, but confinement too in the subjectivity through which one very often learns to survive non-expressive experience. Such notions as 'point of view' or 'voice', while formalised and taught as narrative techniques, are in fact merely lessons in how to exteriorise sensibility, how to make the public persona more consistent with the private, how to put the subjective self to the test of objectivity.

A writer generally has to be alone in order to write: what is interesting about the writing workshop is its communality, suggestive as that is of deficiencies in the social milieu. Alienation produces loneliness, for which, as Marianne Moore said, solitude is the cure. The writing workshop posits a non-alienating social space, and as such creates the possibility of solitude as its sequel; the student who comes to the workshop lonely will leave it, one hopes, ready to be alone.

But to ask the question again: can these endeavours, admirable as they may be, constitute an academic process? What is actually 'taught' in a creative writing class? That these questions are asked so frequently is testament to the mystique of the writing process and the degree to which that mystique is socially owned, an ownership that is part of the democratic ownership of language itself. We resist the idea that writing could be 'technical': the narrative principle is too fused with our experience of living for us to perceive it as a system of rules. Indeed, we believe everyone has a book in them – a book, not a symphony, and not even a poem. What is it, this book everyone has in them? It is, perhaps, that haunting entity, the 'true' self. The true self seeks release, not constraint. It doesn't want to be corseted in a sonnet or made to learn a system of musical notations. It wants liberation, which is why very often it fastens on the novel, for the novel seems spacious, undefined, free. In the novel that common currency, language, can be exchanged like for like. The novel seems to be the book of self: the problem is that, once you start to write it, you see that it has taken on certain familiar characteristics. It begins to seem not true but false, either a recreation of the false self or a failure to externalise the true one. It is a product, your product: in other words, more of the same. How, then, to produce the 'true' writing? 'Writing is drawing the essence of what we know out of the shadows,' writes Karl Ove Knausgaard in *A Death in the Family*. 'That is what writing is about. Not what happens there, not what actions are played out there, but the there itself. There, that is writing's location and aim. But how to get there?'

There is a spirituality, or at least a mysticism, to this statement that it seems to me ought to be embedded at the core of creative writing culture. The desire to be a published author is perhaps no more than a desire to be 'there' permanently, all the time. What the student gets out of a writing workshop is a feeling of being 'there' for a couple of hours, the beginning of a process by which 'there' – writing – can become a more concrete aspect of identity. One way of getting 'there' is by a system of rules that do, broadly speaking, govern narrative construction; increasingly, in my own teaching, I have come to believe that people already know these rules, but only in relation to their own experience.

The natural grasp of form, structure, style and dialogue can be witnessed everywhere in the way we conduct ourselves, and in the high levels of agreement that can be reached about the meaning of this conduct. The smallest child can tell the story of what he did that day, can work out how to make people laugh or how to make them anxious: by repeating his tale he can start to refine it based on the reactions he gets, learn to emphasise some parts and leave out others. The rules of writing are mostly indistinguishable from the rules of living, but this tends to be the last place people look when searching for 'there'. Yet the essence of what we know – all that we know – is what it is like to be ourselves.

'The past is hidden outside the realm,' writes Proust in *Swann's Way*, 'beyond the reach of intellect, in some material object (in the sensation which that material object will give us) of which we have no inkling. And it depends on chance whether or not we come upon this object before we ourselves must die.' The reattachment of the subjective self to the material object is where much of the labour of writing lies – labour because, in this one sense, writing feels like the opposite of being alive. The intangible has to be reversed back into tangibility; every fibre of subjective perception has to be painstakingly returned to the objective fact from whence it came. The temptation is to elude this labour by 'making things up', by escaping into faux-realities or unrealities that are the unmediated projections of the subjective self. This is not the same thing as imagination or inventiveness: the feeling of not believing something you are reading arises not from the fact that it is set in Hogwarts School but from the suspicion that it is pure projection. A writer who knows how to give subjective content an objective form can be as far-fetched as she likes. A writer who doesn't can make even the most creditable things unbelievable.

This labour, which is the labour to manufacture a feeling of reality, is what is taught, or at least analysed, in creative writing classes. Is it a science? Yes, to a degree. A well-written text is like a clock: its face shows an agreed representation of a bodiless element – in this case, time – but if you take its back off you find a mechanism that can be dismantled and readily understood. The writer-teacher can explain that mechanism: as in any field, there are people who do this well and people who do it less well. Do students believe that doing a creative writing degree will turn them into a famous author? Not in my experience. It is a course of study, like any other: it adds, rather than creates, value. It offers space, attention, refinement and respect to people in search of 'there'. More than that, it can offer a humane experience of creative self-exposure, one that the published writer – schooled in the hard knocks of critical reception, or the indifference of the lack of one – might envy.

What creative writing does for students is clear; what it does for writers is less so. Writers become teachers for a number of reasons, though need of money is usually one of them. A desire for social participation might be another, and sheer interest in the subject another. As jobs go, teaching is a good one; in fact, there are writers for whom the absence of a professional 'profile' is a hardship in itself. Like Dick Caramel, they configure writing as a 'career' full of obligations and appointments, in order to ward off the suspicion of amateurism and manage the insecurity of creative freedom. Respectability, for the creative writing teacher, is more easily procured; but the role of teacher, like that of parent, effectively ends what might be called creative unselfconsciousness. The teacher/parent is under pressure to surrender, as the phrase goes, the inner child, to displace it into actual children, to become scheduled and reliable in order to leave the child irresponsible and free. For a writer, who may have fought every social compulsion to 'grow up', whose inner world has been constellated around avoiding that surrender, this is an interesting predicament. Like the child, the creative writing student is posited as a centre of vulnerable creativity, needful of attention and authority. So the writer is giving to others the service he might customarily have given himself. It might make him bigger or it might make him smaller, might betoken richness and maturity or depletion – might represent an increase in self, or might bring about its eventual loss.

How to get there: this is what the student comes to learn, and what the writer has to teach. In the face of such a statement, universities have to – and generally do – remain broad-minded. Creative writing can be made more concrete, but not, truly, formalised, for it proceeds on a basis of negotiation and debate among individuals. It has no template: it is an evolving social form. For this reason, the proper home for it is indeed in an academic institution, which can shelter it as a strand of civilisation, an intellectual precept. All sorts of informal 'academies' – among others the Faber Academy, the Mumsnet Academy, and the *Guardian*'s own creative writing masterclasses – have naturally risen in the

wake of academic creative writing culture, but it is up
to universities to steer that culture, to define and refine
it as it evolves.

At an international writers' seminar recently, the
talk turned during a panel discussion to the subject of
creative writing. A number of foreign novelists were
expressing concern about the anglophone domination
of creative writing provision, towards which overseas
students were being inexorably drawn, even at the
cost of having to express themselves in a language not
their own. They wondered what the consequences of
this trend would be for native literatures, and why their
universities could not validate and run courses themselves. One of them, clearly infuriated by this discussion, suddenly delivered himself of a tirade.

Why, he wanted to know, were writers giving encouragement to this abysmal creative writing trend? Why
were they perpetuating the fallacy that writing can be
taught? Did they really want writing to become a kind
of occupational therapy, a tragic pastime for old ladies
and bored housewives – yes, he repeated, old ladies
and housewives bored of staring out of their windows
all day! By now the audience, composed largely of
women, was in fits of laughter. Many of them had spent
the day attending writing workshops organised around
this public event. Yet the more he denounced them, the
more they laughed: it was easy to put them – and us –
to shame. Thinking about it afterwards, it seemed to me
that this mocking discourse is increasingly becoming

obsolete. In a way, it is a form of cultural self-hatred. It was that writer's own insecurity that required him to distinguish himself from old ladies and housewives, to be the 'real' writer, the centre of attention. He had forgotten to honour the principle of freedom that had permitted him to become who he was. If creating writing culture represents only that – freedom – it is justification enough.

III: CLASSICS AND BESTSELLERS

Edith Wharton

The Age of Innocence

The Age of Innocence was Edith Wharton's last great novel. She wrote it in 1919, at the age of fifty-seven. She was by then a rich and famous author long domiciled in France, whose every emotional and practical link to her native New York had effectively been severed. Nonetheless, America had lain at the heart of her most enduring fictions – as her mentor, the novelist Henry James, cleverly foretold that it would when he advised the young Edith to commit herself to the 'untouched field' of the study of contemporary American life.

But unlike her other major novels, *The Custom of the Country* and *The House of Mirth*, *The Age of Innocence* is not a story of contemporary America. The New York that is its subject was as dead, when Wharton wrote it, as the generation wiped out before her eyes in the fields and trenches of France. And yet, in the devastation and bleakness of 1919, it was the morally constricted, privileged New York of her childhood that Wharton felt drawn to consider, as perhaps many others at that time were considering the vanished world – the lost innocence – of the past. Set in the 1870s, but written through the sober perspective of the war, *The Age of Innocence* is a commentary on the loss of a social era, of a whole mode of life and its attendant ways of being. Wharton's own feelings of discontinuity act, in this novel, as the perfect prism for those of the wider human community as it stood in the wake of an unprecedented destruction of its terrain and values, and in the shadow of the coming modernism. It was, of course, her faculty of capturing the universal in the personal that earned Wharton her writerly riches and fame, and *The Age of Innocence* achieves this synthesis with particular intensity. The novel is both private meditation and public avowal, for Edith Wharton was not alone, at that moment in history, in considering the past to be a place of greater innocence. What the moral value of that innocence was – in the largest as well as the most personal and intimate sense – is the question the novel sets out to answer.

Edith Wharton was born Edith Newbold Jones in 1862, third child (after a twelve-year interval) of George and Lucretia Jones. Her parents were rich, well-to-do denizens of the 'old' New York that is the setting of *The Age of Innocence*, a place that in its rigid proprieties and inflexible notions of class amounted to a microcosm of Victorian England. Yet it is clear that America was far too new a country to tolerate such inflexibility for long, and in her novel *The Custom of the Country* Wharton demonstrates the frailty of this 'old' order in the face of the more vigorous spirit of enterprise and aspiration that was burgeoning unstoppably across America at the turn of the century. 'Old' New York had no muscle by comparison; its only value, in *The Custom of the Country*, lies in the momentary satisfaction yielded to the rich arriviste who succeeds in penetrating and buying up its insubstantial mysteries. The genteel snobs of Wharton's childhood faded away in the glare of new money, or else married into it; New York itself changed and expanded beyond recognition, the quasi-parochial town rapidly devoured by a throbbing, indiscriminate metropolis. It is impossible that Wharton herself should not have felt some sadness at this vanishing of the landscape of her youth, and in the opening paragraph of *The Age of Innocence* she delineates with great precision the complex nature of that emotion. Reporting that the shabby old New York Academy of Music is to be replaced by a new opera house 'which should compete in costliness and splendour with those of the great European capitals', Wharton is careful to note that the 'world of fashion' is slightly afraid of this grand improvement:

> [they were] still content to reassemble every winter in the shabby red and gold boxes of the sociable old Academy. Conservatives cherished it for being small and inconvenient, and thus keeping out the 'new people' whom New York was beginning to dread and yet be drawn to; and the sentimental clung to it for its historical associations, and the musical for its excellent acoustics.

Thus the unmistakable note of tragedy – for the opera house, as the reader of 1920 knew, was built – is sounded with the first appearance of the innocence which is the novel's theme. This 'world of fashion' is innocent indeed: childlike, fearful of change, clinging to its old institutions as the child clings to the security of home. The story that the novel unfolds is calculated to show these children at their absolute worst. Newland Archer, young, carefree, favoured, and of good 'old New York' family, is engaged to May Welland, ditto; an alliance by which their respective (respectable) clans are overjoyed, having silently but implacably required it to occur. Newland Archer is unusual in one respect. Unlike his carefree and favoured contemporaries, he has a troublesome splinter of sincerity in his soul. While considering himself to be gloriously in love with May, he nonetheless suspects that his choice of her was no choice at all; that it was determined, at the deepest level, by the values and expectations of their social and familial habitat. He is reasonably content to be driven and directed by this force, expectation. All the same, he knows that it is a force; and so he wonders, privately, what would happen if he chose to contradict it, while of course never contradicting it in the slightest. Newland considers himself to be superior, somehow, to the men of his acquaintance, 'but grouped together they represented "New York", and the habit of masculine solidarity made him accept their doctrine on all the issues called moral. He instinctively felt that in this respect it would be troublesome – and also rather bad form – to strike out for himself.'

The appearance of a cousin of May's, now called

Ellen Olenska, on Newland's social circuit marks the beginning of a series of events that will test not only Newland but every compartment of his world 'in all the issues called moral'. The fifty-year hindsight of Wharton's narration gives a striking anthropological flavour to her presentation of these events. She had been reading *The Golden Bough* and Freud, and found in the concepts of tribalism and taboo a whole language in which the behaviour of 'good' society towards a woman with neither money nor a home of her own, who has in addition had the temerity to leave her husband, could be expressed. Ellen Olenska, emanating the whiff of scandal and degeneracy that New York vaguely classifies as 'European', has run away from the cruel Count Olenski and returned to her homeland, where she affects to believe that society is kinder and more compassionate – more innocent – than the older, aristocratic civilisation in which she has spent her unhappy married life. 'Everything here is good that was – that was bad where I've come from,' she explains to a riveted Newland Archer, who has been mulling over the 'mysterious authority' of her beauty, so complex and experienced by comparison with May Welland's wholesome, scrubbed prettiness.

Newland, whose vanity it has been to consider himself 'different' from the men of his acquaintance, finds this difference crystallised in the 'otherness' of Ellen Olenska. As he is ineluctably drawn away from the propriety-bound rituals of his own life towards the social and moral ambiguity of hers, his behaviour begins to alert his 'tribe' to a danger threatening their most sacred causes. The hoary old chiefs – the van der Luydens, Mrs Manson Mingott – are mobilised; there is an attempt to integrate Ellen, and hence neutralise her; and Newland's wedding to May is hurried through, against the established 'prehistoric' custom. But marriage to May merely intensifies the taboo – and its attraction – of his feelings for Ellen. He finds May vapid company on their honeymoon, and despairs at the alacrity with which she settles down to the role of housewife on their return. Most of all, Newland's discovery that he is constrained makes the constraint impossible to bear. The 'old New York' he used to look on with slightly patronising fondness has become his unmistakable adversary. He has realised that he is not free.

It is through the character of May Welland that Wharton accomplishes her most masterly portrait of the values – and value – of this vanished society, in whose obsolescence even the reader of 1920 could perceive the ambivalence of the author's tragic design. May is conventional and unimaginative, but she is also ferociously determined as she pits herself against the moral chaos of passion and liberty – and wins. Unlike Newland, May is not motivated by personal desire, by vanity or jealousy. In her behaviour lie the interests of her community and way of life; whereas in Newland's only the self and its urges are considered. The extraordinary dinner-party scene in which these events are concluded, in which May recaptures her husband and presides over Ellen's expulsion from their social world, is the ultimate expression of this group consciousness:

> There were certain things that had to be done, and if done at all, done handsomely and thoroughly; and one of these, in the old New York code, was the tribal rally around a kinswoman about to be eliminated from the tribe . . . [Archer] guessed himself to have been, for months, the centre of countless silently observing eyes and patiently listening ears, he understood that, by means as yet unknown to him, the separation of himself and the partner of his guilt had been achieved, and that now the whole tribe had rallied around his wife on the tacit assumption that nobody knew anything, or had ever imagined anything, and that the occasion of the entertainment was simply May Archer's natural desire to take an affectionate leave of her friend and cousin.

It is necessary, perhaps, to examine Wharton's own experience in those years to comprehend the novel's deeply nuanced conclusion, in which the corpse of that old moral order is looked on with a kind of bewildered awe, its power to control human behaviour now utterly mystifying. As a young woman, Wharton was in love with a man called Harry Stevens, scion of another powerful New York family. Their engagement was announced, but for reasons that are unclear their marriage did not take place. The two young people were resolutely separated by their respective clans and by the social machine, almost, it appears, without being consulted. Shortly afterwards, Harry Stevens tragically died, and Edith consented to a more 'acceptable' marriage with Teddy Wharton, a union whose lack of natural love and passion was to torment her for nearly thirty years, until it became possible for her to divorce him and for her life as a free, rich, independent woman belatedly to begin.

So it is, perhaps, Wharton herself who looks back at the novel's end on all that correctness and self-denial with such powerfully mixed feelings; who views it with hindsight, like Newland Archer, from a world in which the individual is now ascendant, a world where the 'standards that bent and bound' people have vanished like mist. How is one meant to make sense of all that obsolete suffering? How is one meant to feel anything other than victimised and abused, when the 'rules' that entailed so much personal pain turn out not to have been rules after all? At the novel's end Newland Archer is fifty-seven, the age Wharton was when she wrote it. And one can consider his answers to these questions to be hers. To traduce the suffering, he realises, to disrespect it, would be the greatest waste of all. Archer, looking at the new world, offers himself one consolation: that no passion of today's free-and-easy youth could match the intensity of the previous generation's thwarted loves. 'The thing one's so certain of in advance: can it ever make one's heart beat so wildly?' In *The Age of Innocence* Wharton likewise embraces the pleasure and pain of her own early life, the innocence that was its sacrifice, the experience that was its bittersweet fruit.

D. H. Lawrence

The Rainbow

The Rainbow came into the world more or less without literary antecedents. Nothing like it had been written before: Lawrence's novel defined new territories that enabled the representation of human experience to move forward into the modern age. The same, of course, can be said of Joyce's *Ulysses*, with which *The Rainbow* was contemporaneous and with which it shared the fate of being disowned and vilified by the literary establishment and the general public alike. Both were banned immediately, though Joyce's erudition and Lawrence's passion could hardly be more distinct from one another. Though both are books of truth, what yokes them together is in fact mere frankness; frankness about the life of the body in its most pedestrian, its most recognisable, its most universal form.

Lawrence is a writer still identified in the general mind as controversial, and controversial he was, but the highly sexed pornographer of public imagination bears no relation at all to the man whose modes of thought and self-expression still retain the power to provoke violent disagreement. The damage done to his reputation almost a century ago has proved curiously permanent; justice – even the famous overturning of the ban on *Lady Chatterley's Lover* at the Old Bailey in 1960 fixed his libidinous image still more firmly by associating it with the mores of that decade – has an uncanny way of eluding him. It was his tragedy, and it remains his tragedy as each successive generation of readers comes to Lawrence with preconceptions about his life and character that are the very opposite of true. His was a cold, harsh, short life filled with rejection, poverty and sickness, in which every comfort of social, family and intellectual life was denied. That such conditions could produce the supreme work of generosity and empathy that is *The Rainbow* is mysterious and miraculous in equal measure; and indeed the mystery and the miracle of creation is what this literary masterpiece sets out both to evoke and to immortalise in its place at the core of ordinary life.

'One is not only a little individual, living a little individual life,' Lawrence wrote in a letter at the time of *The Rainbow*'s composition. 'One is in oneself the whole of mankind, and one's fate is the fate of the whole of mankind.' The brevity and the vastness of this statement may be taken not only as the exposition of itself but as the articulation of Lawrence's ambitions for his tale of a Nottinghamshire family's generational movement out of a timeless agrarian communality towards the individualism, alienation and selfhood of life in an industrialised society. This was the movement of history itself; the journey of man out of the fields and into the cities, his emancipation from physical labour

by machines, the new forms of mental life this emancipation made possible, the new – often problematic
– possibilities for relating it offered, the changes in relationship itself it provoked. What *The Rainbow* offers
is an account of how the old world became the new,
how the Victorian era gave way to the modern age,
but Lawrence's statement implies far more than this,
both morally and artistically. The Victorian novel routinely used individual characters to emblematise wider
social and geographical realities, to the extent that its
concept of character often strikes the modern reader
as stylised and lacking in reality. Dickens, George
Eliot, Mrs Gaskell: despite their interest in social change,
regionalism, community, the position of women,
these great English novelists have nothing in common
with Lawrence at all. In *The Rainbow* Lawrence does
more than part company with the Victorian modes of
narration – he destroys them by completely invert-
ing the literary and actual function of 'man' as a representative of 'mankind'. 'One is in oneself the whole
of mankind': in this assertion of the total significance
of the self, Lawrence is seeing the future not just of the
novel but of modern Freudian consciousness, and in
the story of the Brangwen family he begins to imagine
what the texture of this consciousness might be.

The Rainbow was originally conceived as a much
longer novel, to be called *The Sisters* and ultimately
written as two novels, the second of which is *Women in
Love*. It is important to note that Lawrence's definitions

of 'man' and 'mankind' at the outset of this project not only incorporated woman but were chiefly preoccupied by her. He regarded his novel as 'do[ing] my work for women, better than the suffrage'. In a letter he wrote in 1913, he remarked: 'It seems to me that the chief thing about a woman – who is much of a woman – is that in the long run she is not to be had. She is not to be caught by any of the catch-words, love, beauty, honour, duty, worth, work, salvation – none of them – not in the long run.' What she wanted was, he said, satisfaction: 'physical at least as much as psychic, sex as much as soul'. In *The Sisters* he set out to unravel 'the woman question' – 'it is *the* problem of the day,' he wrote, 'the establishment of a new relation, or the re-adjustment of the old one, between men and women' – by interrogating the deepest sources of this satisfaction and its denial through the destinies of the two sisters, Ursula and Gudrun Brangwen; an unravelling so lengthy, requiring such a profound investigation of the origins of female character, that one novel could not encompass it. *The Rainbow*, then, is the story of those origins; of woman as the sempiternal life-giver who through time and change is finally driven to give birth to herself.

Anyone encountering Lawrence's prose for the first time will feel the immediate force of its revelations, the density of its character and the totality of its originality. The opening pages of *The Rainbow*, with their evocation of the cyclical harmony of man and beast and land, are among the most memorable in English literature:

They felt the rush of the sap in spring, they knew the
wave which cannot halt, but every year throws forward
the seeds to begetting, and, falling back, leaves the
young-born on the earth. They knew the intercourse
between heaven and earth, sunshine drawn into the
breast and bowels, the rain sucked up in the daytime,
nakedness that comes under the wind in autumn,
showing the birds' nests no longer worth hiding. Their
life and interrelations were such; feeling the pulse and
body of the soil, that opened to their furrow for the grain,
and became smooth and supple after their ploughing,
and clung to their feet with a weight that pulled like
desire, lying hard and unresponsive when the crops were
shorn away. The young corn waved and was silken, and
the lustre slid along the limbs of the men who saw it.

This is provocative writing, sure enough, but provocation is far from Lawrence's aim. Rather, he is serving his
own vision of an original world free of shame, out of
which arises the discord of gender:

The women were different. On them too was the drowse
of blood-intimacy, calves sucking and hens running
together in droves, and young geese palpitating in the
hand while the food was pushed down their throttle. But
the women looked out from the heated, blind intercourse
of farm-life, to the spoken world beyond. They were
aware of the lips and the mind of the world speaking and
giving utterance, they heard the sound in the distance,
and they strained to listen.

In this Eden, too, the woman's curiosity is the driving force that rouses creation from the stasis of repetition. What is the moral status of this curiosity? Is woman wrong to want 'another form of life than this, something that was not blood-intimacy'? It is culture, civilisation, she is drawn to: 'she strained her eyes to see what man had done in fighting outwards to knowledge, she strained to hear how he uttered himself in this conquest, her deepest desire hung on the battle that she heard, far off, being waged on the edge of the unknown.'

Lawrence considers these questions through the medium of English rural life, beginning his story in the small Midlands village of Cossethay just as a canal has been built through it to connect the new collieries, bringing the first signs of the 'commotion' – the violation, in Lawrence's sexual-topographical vision – of industrialisation to the slumberous valley. The Brangwens have farmed there for so long their origins are lost in the mists of time; the men and women of this family, riding the changes of the late nineteenth century and the new dawn of the twentieth, experience its transformations through their very bodies and minds, live out its recalibrations of domestic power, material wealth, urban migration, social ambition, sexual possibility. They become aware of the world beyond the village and beyond England, discover the concepts of freedom and choice; like waves that advance and draw back but are always encroaching they move generationally towards education, culture, self-fulfilment. Ursula and Gudrun Brangwen, the fruit of this long clamber out of stasis and 'blood-intimacy', are deposited by the novel's end on the shores of the twentieth century: frustrated and desirous in equal measure, vibrating to life at its highest pitch, giving voice to themselves out of the long silence of femininity, they are Lawrence's incarnation of modern womanhood. How will they live? How will they find satisfaction? Not in the manner of their mother or their mother's mother, not by means of domestic power: they will no longer serve as the medium through which life begets itself. The 'wave which cannot halt' is to be halted: Ursula and Gudrun realise that to liberate themselves from the cycle of repetition they will require financial independence from men; they will have to educate themselves; they will have to work. And having liberated themselves from men, what relationship with them can they expect to have? Without the context of hearth and home, childbearing, male protection inextricable from female servitude, what will love between a man and a woman be?

These are the questions with which the novel so fascinatingly concludes, questions Lawrence goes on to address in *Women in Love*. But the achievement of *The Rainbow* in creating the conditions for such questions to be asked is momentous. The Old Testament world of Cossethay, with its ceaseless begetting and harvesting, with the rainbow that stands over it as the sign of God's pleasure in the order of his creation, has finally elapsed.

The new world is a world of fundamental disorder, carved into the old like the collieries and roads and railway lines are being carved into the novel's Midlands landscape. It is a world predicated on the potency of the individual, a world that has moved out of the shelter of God's creation and is creating itself. Lawrence's grasp of what kind of future this implies for men and women, for society, for the earth itself, is extraordinarily complex and prescient. And the 're-adjustment of the old relation' between the sexes is an evolution in which we remain embroiled, with all the pleasures and pitfalls Lawrence perceived.

The Rainbow is a novel that retains its transfigurative power of explanation, its capacity to demystify us to ourselves. Not least physically: to read Lawrence is to read with the body as well as the mind. For this he will always be treated with suspicion, with caution, as long as the formation of the human personality is based around the denial or misrepresentation of the sanctity of the body's wants. But Lawrence possessed the bitter knowledge born of his own experience; that originality and truth will always and ever meet with rejection by the common mind. It was to the individual that he addressed himself, for it is as individuals that we read. This is why Lawrence was a writer; and why reading him remains a subversive, transformative, life-altering act.

On Françoise Sagan

It is one of the ironies of the writer's predicament that self-expression can sometimes become fate. The fiction lays a fetter on the life. To the reader, as often as not, it will all seem to be part of the same story. Scott Fitzgerald, for instance, virtually described his own funeral in *The Great Gatsby*. Albert Camus, more eerily, foretold precisely the manner of his death in *La Chute*. Vaguely, the reader comes to see the writer as nothing more than one of his or her own characters: the suspicion that literature occurs entirely within the bounds of personality is confirmed. A kind of disappointment afflicts our feelings about writers, as it does not those about other artists. It is as though they, with their mortal grasp on the faculty of imagination, have crushed our illusions about human destiny. They have described existence, but they have failed to transcend it. They have failed to provide us with a happy ending.

The obituaries that followed Françoise Sagan's death in 2004 were full of the sense of this failure. She had become, we were told, a tragic, pitiable figure: destitute, isolated, tainted by scandal and alcoholism. She had, of course, produced many books, but none as successful and hence as troubling to history as her

first, published when she was just eighteen. In that
book, *Bonjour Tristesse*, she described the hedonism
and amorality of youth, the hedonism and amorality
of well-heeled French intellectuals, the hedonism and
amorality of post-war Europe on the cusp of the sixties.
Not surprisingly, it was the hedonism and the amorality of her life that interested the obituary writers. For
there it was, her fetter, her fate: from this slender, misunderstood novel, and from its young heroine, Céline,
Françoise Sagan never escaped. *Bonjour Tristesse* concludes with a fatal car accident, and three years after
its publication Sagan, whose love of dangerous driving
invariably forms part of the legend of her life, received
severe head injuries when her Aston Martin crashed at
high speed. The disappointment among the obituary
writers that the author did not submit then and there to
her fictional destiny is palpable.

If there is hedonism, if there is amorality in *Bonjour
Tristesse*, then it is of a most artistically proper kind.
Morality, and its absence, is the novel's defining theme:
in this sense Sagan is far more of a classicist than her
existentialist brethren Sartre and Camus. Certainly,
she concerns herself with the twentieth-century problem of personal reality, of the self and its interaction
with behavioural norms, but in *Bonjour Tristesse* those
norms are as much psychical as societal. Céline, a
motherless seventeen-year-old whose permissive, feck-
less father has provided the only yardstick for her values and personal conduct, offers Sagan a particularly

naked example of the human sensibility taking shape. Céline's encounters with questions of right and wrong, and with the way those questions cut across her physical and emotional desires, constitute an interrogation of morality that it is difficult to credit as the work of an eighteen-year-old author. What is the moral sense? Where does it come from? Is it necessary? Is it intrinsic to human nature? Is it possible to lack a moral sense, and if so does that discredit morality itself? These are the questions that lie at the heart of this brief and disturbing novel.

Céline and her father, Raymond, have decided to rent a summer villa on the Côte d'Azur for two months. Raymond is bringing his girlfriend, Elsa, along for the holiday, though Céline is anxious that the reader should not disapprove: 'I must explain this situation at once, or it might give a false impression. My father was forty, and had been a widower for fifteen years.' Notice that it is Raymond who has been bereaved, not Céline herself: she tells us only that she had been at boarding school until two years earlier. Later, she remembers her father's embarrassment at her ugly uniform and plaited hair when he came to collect her from the station. It is as though they had not seen each other in the intervening years; as though Céline, between the ages of two and fifteen, was an orphan. 'And then in the car his sudden triumphant joy because I had his eyes, his mouth, and I was going to be for him the dearest, most marvellous of toys.'

At the villa the trio are contentedly idle. They swim and sunbathe; they are untroubled by the sense of duty or compunction. Raymond does beach exercises to diminish his belly. The beautiful, vapid, red-haired Elsa badly burns her skin. Céline, who has recently failed her exams at the Sorbonne, lies on the beach running sand through her fingers: 'I told myself that it ran out like time. It was an idle thought, and it was pleasant to have idle thoughts, for it was summer.' One day, a young man capsizes his sailing boat in their creek – this is Cyril, an ardent, good-looking, conventional university student who offers to teach Céline how to sail, and is the ideal prospect for a summer romance.

Chance, impulse, happenstance: this is how life unfolds in the unexamined world of Raymond and Céline. They do not concern themselves with order and structure, the imposition of the will, the resistance to certain desires and the aspiration towards certain goals. Even Elsa merely submits to the sun's power to burn her. Is this the correct way to live? The question does not arise; there is no one to ask it. Until, that is, Raymond announces one evening that he has invited a woman named Anne Larsen to stay. The first thing we learn about Anne is that she was a friend of Céline's dead mother. With the mother, the whole lost world of order, nurture and morality is powerfully invoked. Anne, it is clear, is the emissary of that world: 'I knew that once she had come it would be impossible for any of us to relax completely,' says Céline. 'Anne gave a shape to things and a meaning to words that my father and I prefer to ignore. She set a standard of good taste and fastidiousness which one could not help noticing in her sudden withdrawals, her expressions, and her pained silences.' Anne is beautiful, sophisticated, successful; and unlike Céline, Raymond and Elsa, she is an adult, with an adult's power of censure and moral judgement.

Cyril, too, is an adult – he is shocked by Raymond and Elsa's ménage, and apologises to Céline for kissing her. 'You have no protection against me . . . I might be the most awful cad for all you know,' he says, in a most uncad-like way. When Anne arrives, it is clear that she means to take Raymond and Céline in hand. It is clear, too, that she is in love with Raymond, and that Raymond has reached for her in a bid to escape the pleasurable anomie of his circumstances and the childlike emotional world that he inhabits with Céline. Elsa is dispatched; the mature, glacial, controlling Anne is installed. Soon she and Raymond announce their plans to marry; immediately, Anne begins to impose her will on Céline. She orders her to eat more, to study in her room instead of going to the beach, to cease outright her relations with Cyril. Is this love or is it hatred? Is it nurture or is it control? Is it common sense, or the jealousy of a constricted older woman for her uninhibited stepdaughter? Is it what Céline has missed out on by not having a mother of her own, or what her motherlessness has exposed her to?

Sagan records clearly the effect the change in regime has on Céline: 'It was for this I reproached Anne: she prevented me from liking myself. I . . . had been forced by her into a world of self-criticism and guilty conscience . . . For the first time in my life I was divided against myself.' In one sense, then, morality is a form of self-hatred; it is a wound one assuages by wounding others in precisely the same way. But Anne has done something else – she has stolen Céline's father, her one source of unconditional love. Raymond is now 'estranged' from his daughter; he has 'disarmed and abandoned' her. Céline the divided girl is forced into immorality: she wishes to get rid of Anne and regain Raymond. Her actual powerlessness gives rise to fantasies of power, and these thoughts cause her to oscillate between hatred and terrible guilt. Here, then, is another indictment of morality, as it is lived by Anne. Anne has fomented violence in Céline's pacific nature. By controlling and censuring her, and by interfering with her source of love, she has given her the capacity to do wrong.

This is a masterly portrait of primal human bonds and needs that cannot but be read as a critique of family life, the treatment of children and the psychical consequences of different forms of upbringing. One day, Anne locks Céline in her room, after an argument about schoolwork. At first Céline panics, and flings herself at the door like a wild animal. 'It was my first experience of cruelty.' Then her heart is hardened, her duplicity sealed: 'I sat on my bed and began to plan my revenge.' The form this revenge takes occupies the final section of the book, and is almost theatrical in its psychological grandeur. Céline chooses as her tools her father's childishness, Anne's intransigence, Elsa's vanity, Cyril's responsible nature, and with them she forges a plot in which each of the four is utterly at her mercy. As a dramatist she experiences, for the first time, complete power over others. Her plot is tragic and bitter, but it plays uninterrupted to its end. Neither right nor wrong, neither conformity nor permissiveness, neither love nor hatred winds up the victor of this moral battle: it is insight, the writer's greatest gift, that wins.

Sagan's second novel, *A Certain Smile*, is in many ways a sequel to *Bonjour Tristesse*. Several of the familiar themes are there: the search for and betrayal of the lost mother; the double nature of father/lover and lover/brother; the defence of boredom or nothingness as a moral position more truthful than conventionality. Dominique, a law student at the Sorbonne, meets Luc, the married uncle of her boyfriend, Bertrand. Luc and his gentle, kindly wife, Françoise, take Dominique under their wing, for she is uncared-for and alone, the daughter of distant provincial parents rendered more remote by their unassuageable grief over the death some years earlier of 'a son', as Dominique expresses it. Like Céline, Dominique struggles to maintain the dignity of her own reality, to assert its truth, however abnormal other people might claim to find it. 'I was contented enough, but there was always a part of myself, warm and alive, that longed for tears, solitude, and excitement.'

Luc quickly begins to make advances towards Dominique, even as Françoise is enveloping her in mother-love. Dominique profits from their attention, but can find no moral path through it, for the two forms of affection – sexual and parental – are confused. Luc proposes that Dominique come away with him and have a brief affair, at the end of which he will return to Françoise. Once again, the father-figure is identified with an aberrant morality that results in the girl's betrayal of the mother-figure. More importantly, he denies her emotional reality: according to Luc, his affair with Dominique can proceed only on the basis that she does not love him. The nature of love is the novel's central preoccupation. The uncanny maturity that made Sagan's name as a novelist is most strongly in evidence in her fearless and astute portrayal of love as a psychical event that has its roots in family life and the early formation of personality. To the modern reader, Luc's conduct towards Dominique has strong undercurrents of abuse: her violent emotional trauma in the aftermath of the affair, and the novel's exquisitely ambivalent ending in which the subjective death and rebirth of Dominique is described, go far beyond poignancy or even frankness. 'Something is rotten in the state of Denmark!' Dominique finds herself repeating, without knowing why. Sagan's sense of emotional tragedy is indeed that of the great dramatists.

'Much of the time life is a sort of rhythmic progression of three characters,' Sagan said in an interview, shortly before the publication of *A Certain Smile*. In *Bonjour Tristesse*, this structural tenet is illustrated almost sculpturally by Céline's description of the three adults standing on the stairs the night Raymond transfers his affections from Elsa to Anne: 'I remember the scene perfectly. First of all, in front of me, Anne's golden neck and perfect shoulders, a little lower down my father's fascinated face and extended hand, and, already in the distance, Elsa's silhouette.' These two novels, so spare and rigorous, so artistically correct, so thorough in their psychological realism, are the highest expression of the triangular purity of their author's strange and beautiful *esthétique*.

Olivia Manning

The Balkan Trilogy

'I haven't any parents,' says Harriet Pringle, heroine and presiding spirit of Olivia Manning's Balkan Trilogy. 'At least, none to speak of. They divorced when I was very small. They both remarried and neither found it convenient to have me. My aunt Penny brought me up. I was a nuisance to her, too, and when I was naughty she used to say: "No wonder your mummy and daddy don't love you."'

If a project as lengthy and diverse as The Balkan Trilogy can be represented by a few lines, these words of Harriet's are those lines. Indeed, to be able to discover in a small fragment the structure of the whole is one of the hallmarks of a work of art, and in this sense the compendiousness of The Balkan Trilogy is somewhat deceiving. Harriet's impoverished heart is the unvarying leitmotif of its thousand-odd densely filled pages; a nondescript twenty-one-year-old English girl's lack of parental love the central metaphor for war, displacement, cataclysm and the death of the old world in 1940s Europe.

Nevertheless, it is by virtue of this strange and striking parallel that The Balkan Trilogy preserves its freshness and makes its claim to greatness. In these novels we are shown wartime Europe as a world of emotionally stunted men and women, of people starved by the reticence and coldness of their upbringing, of people who have lacked attention and acceptance and love, who have lacked it generationally; a lack so deep in the grain of (English) social institutions and attitudes that only total destruction could erase it. Indifference, injustice, cruelty, hatred, neglect: in The Balkan Trilogy these are the constituents both of personal memory and of social reality, of private unhappiness and of public violence. In Olivia Manning's analogy, war is the work of unhappy children; but while Harriet embodies the darkness of this perception, she represents too the individual struggle to refute it. Harriet's determination – against every provocation – to preserve her marriage, to stay rather than to abandon, to keep instead of smashing, is the novel's other, private war. Manning claimed to be at her happiest when writing of her own life, and the events of the Balkan and Levant trilogies correspond closely to those of the years (1938–46) she spent in Romania, Greece, Egypt and later Palestine with her husband, the socialist R. D. 'Reggie' Smith, who, barred by poor eyesight from military service, worked as a lecturer for the British Council. Guy and Harriet, newlyweds arriving in Romania on the eve of Britain's declaration of war against Germany, are Olivia and Reggie's undisguised alter egos; and the narrative, so naturalistic, so full of incident and coincidence, so detailed, so densely populated with minor characters, confirms that Manning did indeed have a genius for writing at first hand. But her autobiographical presence in these novels is strikingly magnetised by the world: she is here not to describe herself but to witness. Her eye and ear are a match for the large canvas of war; her Bucharest of 1939–40 is riven with unease and changing political values, filled with sundry foreigners – hacks, hangers-on, diplomats, wanderers, profiteers – uncomfortably exposed by the flash of conflict, and it is brought so brilliantly and meticulously to life that by the end the reader feels she could easily find her own way around its chaotic streets and would recognise half the clientele in the English Bar.

Manning's 'people' are more than literary characters: they have the feeling of real beings who happen to find themselves in the narrative frame, like passers-by caught on camera. Indeed, The Balkan Trilogy is frequently so faithful to the sense of lived life that it is often difficult to discern the hand that is shaping it. The prolix conversations of men and the pointed conversations of women, the hours Guy likes to spend discussing politics with his British legation cronies, evenings at restaurants that are sometimes interminably boring and sometimes fun, the configuration of a room, a street, a shopfront, the slow passage of time and season, most of all the way other people come and go, becoming known or half-known, by a process that seems utterly random and yet on which life is dependent at the deepest level for its structure and form: this river of narrative is both the chief beauty and the central mystery of The Balkan Trilogy.

The 'truth' of a writer's experiences is difficult to unravel, but in these novels the striking impassivity of the point of view is the place to look for it. The shaping hand, we realise, is Harriet's; Harriet's is the recondite soul we are occupying; Harriet who watches, who pays attention, yet so rarely draws the drama to herself. When, as readers, we crave some evidence of sensibility from this fictional world, some attention, some disinterested gift of love, it is Harriet's craving we are experiencing. And as we pass from admiration of Guy, lecturer in English literature and incurably sociable socialist, to a profoundly critical disillusion that nonetheless recognises the impossibility of ever rejecting or abandoning him, we are reliving every twist and turn of Harriet's lonely journey of marriage.

What Guy represents in The Balkan Trilogy is the concept of society as the only possible force for good, and as such he is pitted against the emotional individualism represented by Harriet. Guy would give his last penny to a beggar, his last ounce of strength to a stranger in the street; Harriet, on the other hand, wants exclusivity, attention, possession. 'He gave her an illusion of security – for it was, she was coming to believe, an illusion. He was one of those harbours that prove to be too shallow: there was no getting into it. For him, personal relationships were incidental. His fulfilment came from the outside world.' This conflict, of course, is not just Guy and Harriet's: it is the dialectic of the twentieth century, the essence of the struggle to create a new social order. What is interesting is that Guy's dedication to 'the world', and his concomitant refusal to give Harriet the attention she craves, makes her feel 'safe', for it returns her to the original sensation of being unloved. She is constantly being told that Guy is a 'great man', a 'saint', and in this way we come to understand that it is not only Harriet who feels safe with Guy, who experiences emotional need as a form of shame. Other people – a great number of them – feel it too. What Guy (Guy as socialism) represents for them is a kind of extruded subjectivity, whereby 'need' is separated from 'self', and Manning cleverly gives us the reason why such a representation appears virtuous. For Harriet, and those like her, it entails a new discipline of self-renunciation that eerily re-echoes the old; it offers security, or perhaps 'an illusion of security'.

It is in Harriet's relationship with Clarence, a British legation officer in Bucharest and fellow lost soul, that these ideas are explored. When Clarence tries to tell her about his unhappy childhood, Harriet experiences violent feelings of resistance. 'Don't think about it: don't talk about it,' she silently abjures him. 'She knew [Clarence] was one who, given a chance, would shut her off into a private world.' And she has sufficient self-knowledge to understand that in this way he is exactly like her. 'What was it they both wanted? Exclusive attention, no doubt: the attention each had missed in childhood. Perversely, she did not want it now it was offered. She was drawn to Guy . . . and the open world about him.' Later, in an extraordinary scene, Harriet participates in the 'de-bagging' (a public-school prank whereby a person's trousers are forcibly removed) of Clarence at the Pringles' flat, with Guy and Guy's boorish friend David. David, a bully, identifies Clarence as a victim and Harriet finds herself 'caught into the same impulse to ill-treat Clarence in some way'. After Clarence has left, Harriet wonders:

> 'What is the matter with us? Why did we do that?'
> 'It was a joke,' said Guy, though he did not sound sure of what he said.
> 'Really, we behaved like children,' Harriet said and it occurred to her that they were not, in fact, grown-up enough for the life they were living.

As this vast narrative progresses it becomes clear that what these people lack, what stunts them and renders them no more than oversized children, is the transformative experience of love. It is here that Manning's subtle control of her characters is most skilfully demonstrated, for this lack can be detected everywhere in these densely peopled novels. The disloyalty of Guy's colleagues Lush and Dubedat, the moral cowardice of petty officials like Dobson, Sophie Oresanu's attention-seeking, the emotionally stilted kindness of Inchcape or Alan Frewen, most of all the hermetic childlike selfishness of Harriet's bête noire (and Manning's masterpiece) Yakimov: again and again Manning elicits from her reader not scorn but pity for this handicapped race, encourages us to see them as more damaged than monstrous. Manning was a talented painter who once thought she would pursue a career as an artist, and it is often her physical portraits of her characters that convey most powerfully their loneliness. In this world of repressed emotion it is the body that speaks, that sculpts itself into pitiful and sometimes grotesque forms.

> Professor Pinkrose was a rounded man, narrow-shouldered and broad-hipped, thickening down from the crown of his hat to the edge of his greatcoat. His nose, blunt and greyish, poked out between collar and hat-brim. His eyes, grey as rain-water, moved about, alert and suspicious, like the eyes of a chameleon.

Late in the narrative, when Harriet's experience of transformative love finally and briefly comes, she feels it as a demolishing of that formal loneliness, of bodily isolation.

> Their [Harriet's and Charles Warden's] sense of likeness astonished them. It resembled magic. They felt themselves held in a spellbound condition which they feared to injure. Although she could not pin down any overt point of resemblance, Harriet at times imagined he was the person most like her in the world, her mirror image.

Modern readers of The Balkan Trilogy will certainly marvel at it as a technical accomplishment, as a good read, and perhaps even as a meticulous historical document; but its value as a complete chronicle of an important period in the emotional evolution of Western society is likely to strike today's audience most of all. The relationship between institutional representation and personal experience has been reconfigured in our era; the self is ascendant, the concept of duty remote. But we, too, are part of the eternal flux. The personal and the political, peace and war, the individual and the communal, the need and the obligation, the self and its society: all are in motion, just as they always have been. And if readers conclude that ours at least is a more liberated world than Guy and Harriet's, a more expressive and tolerant world, perhaps even a more loving world, they will also have gained a greater sense of how it came to be so, and of the value of that love, so desperately sought, so bitterly fought for.

Eat, Pray, Love

There's a running gag in Elizabeth Gilbert's bestselling memoir of breakdown and recovery, concerning alternative titles she claims to have considered for her book. 'A few times a week,' runs one example, 'Richard and I wander into town and share one small bottle of Thums Up – a radical experience after the purity of vegetarian ashram food – always being careful not to actually touch the bottle with our lips. Richard's rule about travelling in India is a sound one: "Don't touch anything but yourself." (And yes, that was also a tentative title for this book.)'

The book's actual title, *Eat, Pray, Love*, is sincere, almost reverential: the function of the joke is to fumigate that sincerity regularly to allay any suspicion that the author is taking herself too seriously in her use of it. Not to mention the reader – for the words eat, pray and love might in themselves be an invocation of the lost or prohibited pleasures of femininity: hedonism, devotion, sensuality. Without quite knowing why, twenty-first-century woman finds this a powerful trinity to behold on the cover of a book. These monosyllables govern one another by means of an order both consolatory and somewhat foreign to modern female ex-

perience: eating first, loving last, and praying – an activity unpoliticised by the female psyche and one she
might vaguely associate with being cared for – separating
the two like a referee a pair of boxers in the ring.

The three words correspond to the book's three sections. These in turn refer to a highly schematised year of
Gilbert's life, in which she lived consecutively in three
different countries – Italy, India and Indonesia – to ful-
fil that title more or less on demand. In Italy she eats,
in India she lives in an ashram, in Indonesia she finds
physical passion, and nowhere is it suggested that fate
was anything other than malleable to this plan, that *Eat,
Pray, Love* might for instance have turned out to be a
book about Catholicism, the Kama Sutra and Balinese
cookery.

'It wasn't so much that I wanted to thoroughly explore
the countries themselves,' she writes. 'This has been
done. It was more that I wanted to thoroughly explore
one aspect of myself set against the backdrop of each
country, in a place that has traditionally done that one
thing very well. I wanted to explore the art of pleasure
in Italy, the art of devotion in India and, in Indonesia,
the art of balancing the two. It was only later . . . that
I noticed the happy coincidence that all these countries begin with the letter I. A fairly auspicious sign, it
seemed, on a voyage of self-discovery.'

This is the voice of twenty-first-century self-identity:
subjective, autocratic, superstitious, knowing what it
wants before it gets it, specifying even the unknown to

which it purports to be abandoning itself. It is the voice moreover of the consumer, turning other realities into static and purchasable concepts ('tradition', 'the art of pleasure') that can be incorporated into the sense of self. As though by a further extension of the author's all-powerful will, the book has been three different kinds of success: a critical success, a word-of-mouth bestseller, and the holy of holies, the basis of a film starring Julia Roberts. The new edition has a picture of Roberts on the front cover, a little plastic gelato spoon clamped between her lips. Whatever frisson remains, the sight of a 'perfect' woman publicly displaying her greed was evidently judged sufficient at least to shift a few more copies.

The author's claim that she considered other titles is just one example of her expert use of the camouflage of humour. Gilbert's writing propounds a comic cult of female personality, a kind of literary incarnation of the 'best friend'. From the mouth of this witty warrior-woman the female reader is prepared to hear nearly anything, to have her gender secrets, her most private embarrassments, her deepest dissatisfactions disclosed. In 'best friend' language, humour is a culturally approved manifestation of ambivalence, in which the love of life asserts itself over the admission of destructive desires.

Of course, this is a well-worn mode of female literary expression – *Bridget Jones's Diary* is a good example. The writer elects herself a girlish giant-slayer and strides forth into inadmissible regions of feminine experience: armed only with her personal charisma, her wit and her wisecracks, she sets about its taboos and its secret shames. Violent gender-specific emotions – hatred of one's own body, for instance – are recognised in the same moment as being neutralised by humour. Helen Fielding saw the link between herself and Jane Austen, who invented this genre in which the darkest aspects of female passivity and interiority give rise to an elaborated surface of verbal skirmishing. And at the end of it all the author curtsies – she was only joking, after all. It's a pretty performance, in whose echo chambers some readers are wont to discern the reverberation of emotional depths.

Eat, Pray, Love can be placed unequivocally in this tradition. Women like this literature because it alleviates feelings of pressure without the attendant risks of rebellion or change. Nothing is lost or destroyed or interrogated by comedy, or at least not literally. Yet a book is a placement of internal material in public space. The more representative it is of what people personally feel, the more satisfying and necessary its publication.

The difference here is that the feeling and the representation are not quite the same. The suspicion arises that the female reader is being bled of her private tensions, of her rage, of her politics, in order to give the writer the attention she craves. The reader herself becomes the echo chamber; she may return to these tensions depleted by laughing at them, for if she privately experiences repugnance at her own body – for example – as unacceptable, as a form of failure, she will in some sense have betrayed herself by experiencing it publicly as success.

But *Eat, Pray, Love* is more of a conundrum than it seems from this description, and to begin to understand it one has to examine what Gilbert would call the 'backdrop'. The book opens with her as a high-achieving, wealthy 'career girl' in her early thirties, living *au grand luxe* with her husband in the suburbs of New York. 'Wasn't I proud of all we'd accumulated – the prestigious home in the Hudson Valley, the apartment in Manhattan, the eight phone lines, the friends and the picnics and the parties, the weekends spent roaming the aisles of some box-shaped superstore of our choice, buying ever more appliances on credit? I had actively participated in every moment of the creation of this life – so why did I feel like none of it resembled me?' At night she often finds herself in the bathroom crying her eyes out. Why is she so unhappy? She is not sure she loves her husband; she feels obliged to have a baby but doesn't really want one. Her sister, a mother, has said to her (in a textbook example of the comic-ambivalent mode): 'Having a baby is like getting a tattoo on your face. You really need to be certain it's what you want before you commit.'

Crying in the bathroom one night she finds herself praying. She has never been a religious person, she tells us, but her despair is such that she reaches out to this vaguely benign entity – God – and is surprised to discover she feels better. She unearths her own capacity for devotion, or at least finds in 'God' an object that – unlike any of the real or possible objects in her actual life – will satisfy it. Over the next few months she goes about extricating herself from what she doesn't 'want' – at enormous financial and emotional cost – and formulates her elaborate international pan-cultural plan for self-discovery.

What do Gilbert's large, mostly female readership recognise in this rather tortuous, idiosyncratic and frankly fantastical story? There are several possibilities. One is that they venerate her for reintroducing the idea of the pleasure principle into female experience. She writes as a woman of thirty-five, an age by which many of her readers will be married, to husbands they may experience – in her compelling description – as 'my lighthouse and my albatross in equal measure'; will be wearing that facial tattoo, motherhood; will be shackled to houses of greater or lesser grandeur; will spend their free time with friends or in superstores – and will find their capacity for devotion exploited to the full by their sense of loyalty to these undertakings, their belief that they ought to honour their responsibilities and make the best of the life they've chosen for themselves, even if they sometimes feel that none of it resembles them.

Such a woman is never far from the necessity to cook or abstain from food, to perform an unselfish act, to exercise tolerance and self-sacrifice in relationships that define the core of our cultural conception of love. And she may feel, in the performance of this role, the emotional extremity Gilbert attributes to herself. To have these ordinary aspects of her life repackaged as pleasurable gives her a kind of mental lift; and as Nigella Lawson has discovered, selling the pleasure concept to overcommitted women is big business.

The problem lies in the egotism of these female goddesses and gurus, who require their (female) audience to stand still while they twirl about, who require us to watch and listen, to laugh at their jokes, to admire their beauty and their reality and their freedom, to witness their successes. Elizabeth Gilbert is a relentless cataloguer of such successes, social, gastronomic, spiritual and sexual: the pizza she eats in Naples, the lover she takes in Bali, the friends she makes, even the quality of her transcendence at the ashram, all are perfect, the very best.

This voyage of self-discovery, it turns out, was a competition, at whose heart is a need to win. Gilbert refers once or twice in her book to a childhood in which she was driven to do well and achieve, and her failure to reconcile the forced fruits of female ambition with the realities of woman's destiny merely embroiders further the space between the two. Her Damascene epiphany in her New York bathroom might have led her not to break the life she had but to accept it, to exercise her capacity for devotion right there; she might have gone to Italy not to eat pasta but to acquire knowledge;

she might have chosen not to live entirely and orgias-tically in the personal – in pleasure – but instead to have renounced those interests in pursuit of a genuine equality.

But to say that, of course, would be to take it all much too seriously.

Never Let Me Go

In Kazuo Ishiguro's 1995 novel *The Unconsoled*, Ryder, a pianist, is due to give an important concert in a foreign city. The novel is written in the form of an extended anxiety dream: manifold impediments spring up to delay his arrival at the concert hall; at one point he realises he hasn't practised the pieces he intends to play. In a field outside the city where, through labyrinthine causes, he finds himself, he comes across the dilapidated wreck of his old childhood family car. 'I stared through the spiderweb cracks [in the window] into the rear seat where I had once spent so many contented hours. Much of it, I could see, was covered with fungus.' The elasticity of the subconscious is also the novel's elasticity – it is more than five hundred pages long – and likewise the novel's procedures are those of its adopted system of Freudian values.

This tendency – which might be called a type of impersonation, a kind of camouflaging of the writer's authority and hence his responsibility – can be seen throughout Ishiguro's work, and goes hand in hand with his most persistent themes: the fear of disorganisation and abandonment; the psychical aftermath of childhood; and the relationship between the institutional and the personal through which these themes are frequently dramatised. His most popular novel, *The Remains of the Day*, recommended itself to readers by the purity of its translation of that perennial English favourite, the period piece: here the author's lack of presence was felt to be impeccable, as discreet and thorough as the butler himself, serving up an England of which he didn't personally partake. But impersonation is also hubris, arrogance, control, for it seeks to undermine or evade the empathetic basis of shared experience. Without empathy, the impersonator can misjudge people quite as spectacularly as he second-guesses them: in Ishiguro's case, *The Unconsoled* bewildered and alienated the very readers *The Remains of the Day* had gone to such lengths to satisfy. And indeed, *The Unconsoled* can on one level be regarded as a sort of outburst, almost an act of personal aggression, though it is a lengthy and meticulous work.

Never Let Me Go is Ishiguro's sixth novel and has proved to be his most popular book since his Booker Prize–winning heyday. As with *The Remains of the Day*, there is a film, replete with English celebrities. Ishiguro's ventriloquism announces itself in the novel's first lines: 'My name is Kathy H. I'm thirty-one years old, and I've been a carer now for over eleven years. That sounds long enough, I know, but actually they want me to go on for another eight months, until the end of this year.' The 'now' and the 'actually', the absorbed ordinariness, the vagueness of 'they' and the precision of 'eight months, until the end of this year': Ishiguro's ear is acute, and these are the verbal mannerisms of the public services sector in the humdrum modern world. Kathy is a 'carer', and indeed the notion of the 'caring professions' represents precisely that elision of the institutional and the personal that generates the undertone of disturbance in so much of his work. There are undertones of Kafka, too, in these words, and in the immediate sense they convey of the reader's imprisonment in the narrator, and thus of the narrator's actual powerlessness. Another elision is the humdrum and the sinister: triviality is the harbinger of evil, and Ishiguro's prose from the outset is conspicuously dull with trivia. Kathy calls the people she cares for 'donors', and on the third page she says of one of them: 'He'd just come through his third donation, it hadn't gone well, and he must have known he wasn't going to make it.' And so the association, the elision, is swiftly clarified. This is a book about evil, the evil of death, the evil of banality: 'he must have known he wasn't going to make it.'

Never Let Me Go takes place in the late twentieth century, in an England where human beings are cloned and bred for the purposes of harvesting their organs once they reach adulthood. These 'clones' are reared in boarding school-type institutions: much is made, in the clone community, of the differences between one institution and another. Hailsham, where Kathy grew up as an inmate before her 'promotion', is mythologised for its special ethos: a Hailsham childhood is idealised, with somewhat grotesque and faintly Dickensian sentimentality, by those who were 'born' into less fortunate circumstances. Hailsham is a grand place whose ample grounds encompass a pond, a pavilion and, towards its perimeter fence, a sinister area known as 'the woods'. It is staffed by 'guardians' who have the quasi-parental function of the boarding-school housemaster or -mistress: these worthies bear the knowledge of their charges' fate as best they can. Once the children have reached maturity they leave their school-type community and embark on a twi-lit adult life, in which they are given limited access to the normal world while they await the summons to make their first 'donation'. This is where Kathy, as carer, comes in: she is the attending angel, seeing her portfolio of donors through the series of operations and consequent deteriorations that will lead to their certain death, or 'completion'. This role has extended her own lease on life, and so she must endure the survivor's moral and emotional suffering. And in-deed, it is her capacity for emotion that provides the narrative occasion, that makes her the writer of this account.

It would seem from this description that *Never Let Me Go* is a work of unremitting bleakness and gratu-itous sordidness. At the very least the question might be asked what style of literary enterprise this is. It isn't science fiction – indeed its procedures are the very reverse of generic, for there is no analogy at work in the text, which instead labours to produce its iterative naturalism as a kind of subset or derivation of our own. In this sense it has more in common with a novel such as Camus's *The Plague*, in which a dystopian but familiar reality dramatises the dilemmas of the age. But the dilemmas of our age are not really those of Ishiguro's dystopia: vainglorious science, meddling with the moral structure of life, is a kind of B-list spook whose antics have yet to offer any substantial intellectual or practical challenge to the populace.

In any case, the 'scientific' basis of the novel is vague: it is the emotional world of the clones themselves that Ishiguro is interested in, for these are children without parents, children who lack the psychological burden of childhood that Ishiguro so painstakingly articulated in *The Unconsoled*. And what he concludes is that a child without parents has no defence against death; that its body is not sacred, that it is a force of pure mortality. The parent is a kind of god, sanctifying and redeeming the child: as in Cormac McCarthy's *The Road*, the novel's horrific imaginings almost become a perverse kind of sentimentality, as though these (male) writers are unable entirely to distinguish between imagination and fear. The parent imagines the gruesome things that could happen to his child if he, the parent, weren't there to protect him; and the novelist tries to translate those imaginings into the empirical evidence valued by male literary culture. He creates a 'reality' out of them, with every ghoulish component unrelentingly worked out and provided; a high-caste version of the tabloid newspaper's loving exposition of gory detail.

The Road has also been a popular success: readers seem to find the depressiveness of these novels exhilarating. In Ishiguro's case the 'gory details' of organ donation and human exploitation are further freighted with the artistic scruples of the impersonator. The prose is locked tight with the inescapable repetitions of reminiscence: 'There's an instance I can remember from when we were about eleven. We were in Room 7 on a sunny winter's morning. We'd just finished Mr Roger's class, and a few of us had stayed on to chat with him.' The greater part of the narrative proceeds thus, and Ishiguro gets his darkest effects from this 'dead hand' approach, creating an atmosphere of unbearable constriction that is like looking back down a tunnel. But his simultaneous need to manipulate, to dramatise his own concerns, pulls the story in the opposite direction. He gives the world of Hailsham a dominant characteristic: the belief in, indeed the worshipping of, creativity. The Hailsham children are indoctrinated in – and, one suspects as the narrative progresses, deliberately blinded by – the belief that their personal worth and the meaningfulness of their lives resides entirely in their ability to create art. From their earliest years they paint and sculpt and write poetry; they 'sell' their work to one another at passionate auctions known as 'Exchanges'; the cream of the school's production is selected to be sent to 'the Gallery', by a woman known as Madame, who comes two or three times a year in her smart clothes to make her choices. Kathy's friend Tommy, though highly talented at sport, is bullied and ostracised for being bad at art; when he tells her that one of the guardians has privately suggested to him that his artistic failure doesn't matter, she hears this as the cataclysm of heresy.

On one level Ishiguro seems to be saying that art is a con-trick, like religion; that it obscures from us the knowledge or awareness of our own mortality, knowledge that in the case of the Hailsham children is brutally withheld. We believe that art is immortal, and so we represent creativity as an absolute good; but in making this representation to children, are we interfering with their right to know about and accept death?

At one point Kathy remembers the way poems were treated as equivalent to paintings or sculptures at the Exchanges: it seems strange to her now that it should have been so. 'We'd spend precious tokens on an exercise book full of that stuff rather than on something really nice for [putting] around our beds. If we were so keen on a person's poetry, why didn't we just borrow it and copy it down ourselves any old afternoon?' Ishiguro's mask slips a little here: why go to such lengths to distinguish and devalue writing? Is he suggesting that this is what the culture does? Or is it the reverse, a further piece of evidence of the inside-out, perverted values of the novel's world?

Never Let Me Go, like the clones it portrays, has in the end something of a double nature, for it both attracts and annihilates. Or perhaps it is a book that requires two readers, the reader who can be blind to its ugly visage, and the reader who can see into its delicately conflicted soul. For those who perceive the latter, the novel's bleak horror will leave a bruise on the mind, a fetter on the heart.

On Natalia Ginzburg

The voice of the Italian novelist and essayist Natalia Ginzburg comes to us with absolute clarity amid the veils of time and language. Writings from more than half a century ago read as if they have just been – in some mysterious sense are still being – composed. No context is required to read her: in fact, to read her is to realise how burdened literature frequently is by its own social and material milieux. Yet her work is not abstract or overtly philosophical: it is deeply practical and personal. You come away from it feeling that you know the author profoundly, without having very much idea of who she is.

It isn't quite right to call these contradictions, because they are also the marks of a great artist, but in this case perhaps it is worth treating them as such, since they enabled Ginzburg to evolve techniques with which contemporary literature is only just catching up. Chief among these is her grasp of the self and of its moral function in narrative; second – a consequence of the first – is her liberation from conventional literary form and from the structures of thought and expression that Virginia Woolf likewise conjectured would have to be swept away if an authentic female literature were to be born. Yet this liberation is entirely towards naturalness and simplicity; it is an advance made without the propulsive force of ego, and so it is easy not to recognise it as an advance at all. Finally, Ginzburg gives us a new template for the female voice and an idea of what it might sound like. This voice emerges from her preoccupations and themes, whose specificity and universality she considers with a gravitas and authority that seem both familiar and entirely original. It is an authority grounded in living and being rather than in thinking or even in language, an authority perhaps better compared to that of the visual artist, who is obliged to negotiate first with the seen, tangible world.

Ginzburg was born in Palermo in 1916, the child of a Jewish father and Catholic mother. Theirs was a left-wing intellectual household and she grew up into a milieu of radical thinkers and writers who became, with the advent of war, the defenders of liberalism and free speech. She and her young husband, Leone Ginzburg, were part of a group of anti-fascist activists and were central figures in protecting the freedom of the press. As well as essays Ginzburg wrote several novels, the most famous of which, *Family Lexicon*, is a history of a family whose observational core – in the person of its narrator and daughter of the family, Natalia – remains opaque. Ginzburg's distinctive writing technique is easier to analyse in the more spacious setting of the novel. What at first might seem to be a narrative strategy, whereby Natalia withholds her own thoughts and feelings while her observations of those around her pour forth, becomes a profound commentary on the nature of narrative itself and how it so often misrepresents the trauma and tragedy inherent in living. Ginzburg separates the concept of storytelling from the concept of the self and in doing so takes a great stride towards a more truthful representation of reality. She identifies narrative as being in some important sense a bourgeois enterprise, a gathering of substance from the world in order to turn it to the story's own profit, and moreover a process of ineradicable bias, whereby things only become 'real' once they have been recognised and given value by an individual. Put simply, Ginzburg attempts to show what happened without needing to show it happening to somebody. Her job – her art – is to represent the flawed charm, the tragedy and comedy of the human, to show the precise extent to which our characters shape our destinies and to watch as those destinies confer their blows and their rewards upon us.

The essays in *The Little Virtues*, written separately and in distinct circumstances between 1944 and 1960, comprise an autobiography of sorts. 'Winter in the Abruzzi' describes a period in which the author, then a young wife and mother, was exiled in wartime with her family to the Italian countryside. In 'Worn-out Shoes' she is now alone, living in post-war Rome with another solitary woman, her children being taken care of by her mother outside the city. 'My Vocation' describes the dawning of her realisation that creativity is a lifetime calling and is the most enduring of the relationships she will have. In 'England: Eulogy and Lament' she is older and exiled again, this time in a strange country whose manners and mores she records by way of making an inventory of her own homesickness and sorrow. In 'He and I' she is living with a man whose character she can only describe in terms of its differences from her own, in what is palpably a relationship of middle age; this time the sense of exile is emotional as well as geographical, the feeling of alienation from one's own history that comes from living with a man who is not the father of one's children. 'The Little Virtues', a work of great restraint and courage, is a look back at parenthood. Entirely without sentiment or subjectivity, it identifies the moral cowardice inherent in conventional attitudes to children and their upbringing, and the ways in which we inculcate the values of materialism and selfishness in the generations that will replace us. 'As far as the education of children is concerned I think they should be taught not the little virtues but the great ones. Not thrift but generosity and an indifference to money; not caution but courage and a contempt for danger; not shrewdness but frankness and a love of truth; not tact but love for one's neighbour and self-denial; not a desire for success but a desire to be and to know.' This statement of principle serves equally as a description of Ginzburg's own life and work.

Among the many themes touched on by Ginzburg –

war, relationships, loss, belief, domesticity, art – the matter of femininity is handled with surprising under-statement and reserve. The author occupies the suc-cessive roles of daughter, wife, mother and partner without ever allowing her perspective to be subsumed into them. Yet she is perfectly honest about what the playing of these roles involves. 'And then my children were born,' she writes in 'My Vocation', 'and when they were very little I could not understand how any-one could sit herself down to write if she had children. I did not see how I could separate myself from them in order to follow someone or other's fortunes in a story.' She describes the pitfalls of gender – both male and female – without ever falling into them. This unusual objectivity, achieved by a careful use of distance that is never allowed to become detachment, is one of the pleasures of reading Ginzburg; yet it perhaps bears greater examination as an example of how a woman writer might make and inhabit an authentic place for herself in the world. 'Irony and nastiness seemed to be very important weapons in my hands,' she writes of her early attempts to create stories; 'I thought they would help me write like a man, because at that time I wanted terribly to write like a man and I had a horror of anyone realising from what I wrote that I was a woman.' She goes on to describe how the acceptance of her woman-hood was fundamental to her birth as an artist, but she is careful to point out that this was not conscription to a gendered view of life: rather, it was the self-acceptance crucial to enabling anyone to speak with their own voice. The basis of Ginzburg's world view is equality, and the stories that are built on it are built from the formation and function of individual human character alone. Here, morality and the choices that are consequent on it are the engine of narrative.

'My husband died in Rome,' she writes at the end of 'Winter in the Abruzzi', 'in the prison of Regina Coeli, a few months after we left the Abruzzi. Faced with the horror of his solitary death, and faced with the anguish which preceded his death, I ask myself if this happened to us – to us, who bought oranges at Giro's and went for walks in the snow.' The torture and murder of Leone Ginzburg by the fascist police, the destruction through war of the known reality, the loss of the world of childhood and the breaking of its concept of authority: these things 'happened' to Natalia Ginzburg and it seems they taught her much about the dangers of extremity both to human character and to art. The exceptional violence and pain of her experiences are painstakingly transmuted into a clear-eyed universality where cruelty and exaggeration, even if they have their basis in fact, are not tolerated.

'And you have to realise that you cannot console yourself for your grief by writing . . . Because this vocation is never a consolation or a way of passing the time. It is not a companion. This vocation is a master who is able to beat us till the blood flows . . . We must swallow our saliva and tears and grit our teeth and dry the blood from our wounds and serve him. Serve him when he asks. Then he will help us up on to our feet, fix our feet firmly on the ground; he will help us overcome madness and delirium, fever and despair. But he has to be the one who gives the orders and he always refuses to pay attention to us when we need him.'

Acknowledgements

The essays in this collection have been published previously or are forthcoming:

'Driving as Metaphor' (*New York Times Magazine*); 'Coventry' (*Granta*); 'On Rudeness' (*New York Times Magazine*); 'Making Home' (*New York Times Magazine*); 'Lions on Leashes' (*New York Times Magazine*, as 'Raising Teenagers: The Mother of All Problems'); 'Aftermath' (*Granta*); 'Louise Bourgeois: *Suites on Fabric*' (Marlborough Fine Art Exhibition Catalogue essay); 'I Am Nothing, I Am Everything' (*The Last Supper*, Faber & Faber, 2010); 'Shakespeare's Sisters' (*Guardian*); 'How to Get There' (*Guardian*); 'Edith Wharton: *The Age of Innocence*' (Introduction, *The Age of Innocence*, The Folio Society, 2009, and Macmillan Collector's Library, 2019); 'D. H. Lawrence: *The Rainbow*' (Introduction, *The Rainbow*, Vintage Classics, 2011, republished in the *Guardian*); 'On Françoise Sagan' (Introduction, *Bonjour Tristesse*, Penguin Modern Classics, 2013); 'Olivia Manning: The Balkan Trilogy' (Introduction, *Fortunes of War: The Balkan Trilogy*, Olivia Manning, New York Review of Books Classics, 2010); '*Eat, Pray, Love*' (*Guardian*); '*Never Let Me Go*' (*Guardian*); 'On Natalia Ginzburg' (*Times Literary Supplement* and Introduction, *The Little Virtues*, Daunt, 2018).